A PHENOMENOLOGY
OF PENTECOSTAL
LEADERSHIP

A PHENOMENOLOGY OF PENTECOSTAL LEADERSHIP

Truls Åkerlund

WIPF & STOCK · Eugene, Oregon

A PHENOMENOLOGY OF PENTECOSTAL LEADERSHIP

Wipf & Stock
An Imprint of Wipf and Stock Publishers
199 W. 8th Ave., Suite 3
Eugene, OR 97401

www.wipfandstock.com

PAPERBACK ISBN: 978-1-5326-3979-1
HARDCOVER ISBN: 978-1-5326-3980-7
EBOOK ISBN: 978-1-5326-3981-4

Manufactured in the U.S.A.

To her.
Who calls it a dance when I clumsily lead her over the kitchen floor
on a rainy Saturday morning. Who makes our house a home, our
arguments frustrating, and our marriage a joy.
Who for several years has patiently (and at a times impatiently!) shared
my attention with German men with incomprehensible ideas and long
beards. Honey, I swear they are back on the shelf now.

To Gro.
Without your support this project would never been realized.
I love you!

Contents

Acknowledgements

WHILE I TAKE THE sole responsibility for the results and claims of this work, others are included to share whatever praise it deserves. In addition to my wife, my deepest appreciation goes to our sons, Benjamin, Joel, and Aron. Thank you for bearing with my constant nagging about new research on this and that and for keeping me culturally savvy. It has been and still is the joy of my life to see you grow from boys to men, children to friends. I am forever thankful to my extended family, who never really grasped what I was working on but supported me nonetheless—especially to my late grandmother, Marit Fjeld Ingebrethsen, who always pictured me a doctor, albeit of the more medical type.

To colleagues and friends at the Norwegian School of Leadership and Theology: Thank you all for steadfast encouragement and support, financially as well as academically and personally. I am particularly indebted to Karl Inge Tangen for great conversations and much laughter, and for you being a role model in combining academic rigor with spiritual passion and sensitivity; to Bente Sandtorp for more laughter and corporation in teaching and ministry; and to Kai Tore Bakke and the Board of Trustees for giving me the opportunity to embark on doctoral studies as a part of my work obligations. This study would never be realized had it not been for this opportunity.

A special thanks goes to the faculty and staff at Regent University's School of Business and Leadership for their generous support and encouragement, particularly to Corné Bekker for directing my curiosity, handling my frustrations, and celebrating my wins. Gratitude to Hennie Van der Mescht of Rhodes University, South Africa, for taking the time to share your experiences and discuss phenomenological bracketing with a novice Norwegian phenomenologist. Thanks also to Giorgi Amedeo, Frederick Wertz, Magnus Englander, Idun Røseth, Rob Bongaardt, and Olav

Tangvald-Pedersen for personally helping my find my way in the maze of phenomenological methodology.

Thanks to my mentors and friends: to Joseph Umidi for shaping my philosophy of ministry; to Øystein Gjerme for providing an example of how to combine critical thinking and constructive ministry; to Egil Svart-dahl for lending an ear and stretching out a hand; and to other pastors and friends in the Pentecostal movement for stirring my appetite for ecclesial leadership and inviting me into their lives to study and learn from it. And above all:

> God, the blessed and only Ruler, the King of kings and Lord of lords, who alone is immortal and who lives in unapproachable light, whom no one has seen or can see. To him be honor and might forever. Amen. (1 Tim 6:15–16)

Introduction

ACCORDING TO HISTORIAN Vinson Synan, the twentieth century was the century of the Holy Spirit.[1] From its humble beginnings in the ghettoes of Los Angeles, Pentecostalism has evoked the largest shift on the global religious scene over the last decades—with research estimating more than 640 million Pentecostal/Charismatics worldwide in 2015.[2] Despite the frequent references to divine providence and denial of any human contributions, Wacker contends that strong leadership has been an important ingredient of the Pentecostal movement from its very beginning:

> If the essence of leadership was the ability to persuade people to do what needed to be done, the essence of effective leadership was the ability to persuade them to do it of their own accord. And in this respect the revival's torchbearers proved skillful beyond their grandest dreams.[3]

Other observers concur and suggest that the astonishing growth of global Pentecostalism may partly be attributed to the movement's entrepreneurial leaders and preachers.[4]

Given this prominent role of leadership and the numerous examples of famous and infamous Pentecostal leaders, it is quite surprising to learn how little is actually written on the topic of Pentecostal leadership. A title scan of published articles in major academic journals on Pentecostalism reveals that only sixteen of more than twelve hundred studies specifically

---

1. Synan, *Century of the Holy Spirit.*

2. Johnson et al., "Christianity 2015," 29.

3. Wacker, *Heaven Below,* 141.

4. Anderson, *To the Ends of the Earth,* 224; Nelson, "Authority, Organization, and Societal Context," 672.

address issues of leadership.[5] This clearly illustrates how leadership is, to a large extent, ignored in Pentecostal studies to date. As is evident from the literature review in Part 1 of this book, the picture is not as grim as the article search assumes. Scholars inside and outside the Pentecostal community have discussed issues of power, influence, and charisma, and research specifically addressing Pentecostal leadership is emerging. Yet, Burns's maxim that "we know all too much about our leaders, we know far too little about *leadership*" still holds true for leadership in the global Pentecostal movement.[6] In Heuser and Klaus' words,

> Our inquiry into the state of Pentecostal leadership is less docu-
> mented [than Pentecostalism's quantitative growth] and may yield a
> wide range of discussions in attempts to interpret such messy reali-
> ties. It is reasonable to expect certain characteristics of leadership to
> exist (for better or worse) in Pentecostal-charismatic leadership due,
> at least in part, to an ideology which shapes the tradition.[7]

It is these characteristics the present study sets out to explore.

The notion that leadership changes in context is addressed from various angles and paradigms, such as cultural, religious, constructivist, institutional identity, and sense-making perspectives.[8] Though these approaches
represent at times incompatible perspectives on leadership vis-à-vis each
other, they agree that leadership varies in different contexts. This must be
kept in mind when studying leadership in ecclesial settings. The steady
stream of research addressing leadership from confessional or denominational angles reflects this awareness—one prominent example being Callahan's reference handbook on religious leadership, which treats leadership in

5. The result is based on a scanning of all titles ($N = 1,272$) of peer-reviewed articles in *Journal of Pentecostal Theology*, *Pneuma*, *Asian Journal of Pentecostal Studies*,
Australasian Pentecostal Studies, *Pentecostudies*, and *Canadian Journal of Pentecostal-
Charismatic Christianity* in August 2015. The total number of articles is debatable, as
different journals use different headings to distinguish between research articles and
other genres. In a similar way, it might be argued that more articles discuss issues of
leadership in addressing topics such as power, institutionalization, gender issues, etc.
None of these elements changes the conclusion, however, that the ratio between the total
numbers of articles and those discussing leadership reveals that Pentecostal leadership is
an under-researched area.

6. Burns, *Leadership*, 1.

7. Heuser and Klaus, "Charismatic Leadership Theory," 167.

8. E.g., Weber and Glynn, "Making Sense with Institutions"; Dorfman et al.,
"GLOBE"; Shah, "Re-thinking Educational Leadership"; Osborn et al., "Toward a Contextual Theory"; Glynn, "Beyond Constraint."

various religious and confessional contexts separately rather than lumping them together as if they represent one uniform phenomenon.[9] The implicit premise is that leadership takes on distinct meanings and flavors in various religious contexts.

While churches certainly are "organizations that are subject to the pressures and exhibit the characteristics of organizations,"[10] the *ecclesia* constitutes a special kind of organization with a distinct *raison d'être*. It is in many ways a child of two mothers—born of heaven and born of earth, so to speak—having both theological and sociological foundations and manifestations. To keep spirituality and administration in balance is thus a constant challenge for ecclesial leadership, one that may be solved by means of a religiously rooted normativity.[11] Consequently, one cannot simply assume that general leadership theories apply in ecclesial contexts, as they do elsewhere.

As Stewart points out, traditional organizational leadership research may at times describe and prescribe behaviors that are inconsistent with underlying assumptions in ecclesial organizations.[12] This is not to say that congregational leaders should refrain from learning from general leadership research. Rather, the argument makes a case for research that takes the dynamics of ecclesial leadership—in context—seriously by asking questions and using methodology that allow for its distinctiveness to surface. In this regard, observers of Pentecostalism warn about using categories and frameworks from other streams of research to describe the movement, as they may fall short in accounting for its unique character.[13]

Take, for instance, the use of Max Weber's theory of charismatic leadership, which is a frequent companion in studies of Pentecostalism. Nelson notes that, although charisma may be a prominent organizing principle within Pentecostalism, it plays out differently in different contexts with minimal uniformity internationally and with considerable influence from the wider social environment.[14] Further, Tangen points to the risk of downplaying theological aspects of charisma if relying too much on sociological

---

9. Callahan, *Religious Leadership*.

10. Sturgill, "Church Web Sites," 168.

11. Ershova and Hermelink, "Current Church Organization," 241–42.

12. Stewart, "Workplace," 305–6.

13. Cartledge, "Practical Theology," 282; Smith, *Thinking in Tongues*, loc. 268.

14. See Nelson, "Authority, Organization."

explanations in studies of Pentecostalism.[15] In short, it is beneficial to study leadership in Pentecostalism on its own terms—as it is experienced by the leaders in the movement. This is the road taken in the present work.

Purpose and Significance of the Study

There are personal and academic reasons to embark on this study. To begin with the first, I am a Pentecostal, exercise leadership at various levels in Pentecostal churches, teach at a school partly owned by a Pentecostal church, and provide education in leadership and theology from a Pentecostal perspective. As such, I am deeply involved in the topic addressed in this study, and my experiences of Pentecostal leadership in addition to my previous work on the topic have stirred the appetite to better understand the dynamics of leadership in Pentecostalism.[16] Of particular interest is the paradoxical and, at times, perplexing fusion and/or conflict between pragmatism and primitivism, pneumatology and leadership theory, empowerment of marginalized groups and power to the anointed few.

However, these issues go beyond mere personal interest, as there are several reasons to study Pentecostal leadership from a scholarly perspective. First, the disproportionality between the growth of Pentecostalism and the relative lack of interest in leadership within its ranks speaks for an intensifying of research on the phenomenon in the years to come. While global Pentecostalism has changed the religious landscape of the world, our understanding of its leadership lags behind and draws largely on constructs imposed from other settings and contexts. By explicating and describing essential characteristics of Pentecostal leadership, the present work seeks to fill a void in the extant literature. While its primary aim and scope is academic, the study has the potential of contributing to more robust and healthy forms of leadership in Pentecostal organizations by bringing to the surface leadership dynamics that often remain tacit or hidden. To address such issues, I believe, is a necessary part of Pentecostalism's ongoing journey into adulthood. In the last decades of the twentieth century, Pentecostal scholars were arguing that the movement was at a crossroad,[17]

15. Tangen, "Karismatisk Ledelse," 228–33.

16. See Appendix A for a brief discussion on possibilities and problems related to my proximity to the phenomenon.

17. Cox, *Fire from Heaven*, 309–10; Faupel, "Whither Pentecostalism"; Poloma, *Assemblies of God*.

"experiencing a turbulent adolescence characterized by a search for new identity."[18] A common concern was that Pentecostalism indeed has something to offer to the church and the world but that, to do so, Pentecostals must wrestle with their own characteristics and identities. Warrington lists issues related to leadership among the most significant challenges that needed to be addressed in the movement, and fears that "the Pentecostal revival will slow down and even implode if these aspects [leadership, personal spirituality and a moral framework] are not seriously examined and conclusions carefully implemented."[19] A goal of this study is therefore to illuminate the dynamics of Pentecostal leadership, a phenomenon that has received proportionately little attention, given the exceptional growth of the Pentecostal movement.

Second, by exploring experiences of Pentecostal leadership, the present work may shed light on organizational dynamics that are rarely addressed in mainstream management research. The religious soil is arguably ripe with leadership insights, not only for religious organizations but also for the wider field of organizational studies. In a fairly recent conference, leading management scholars, including Peter Senge, Christ Agyris, and Henry Mintzberg, called on theology (among other disciplines) to develop a new philosophical foundation for Management 2.0.[20] In a similar vein, Dyck and Wiebe argue for a theological turn in management research—witnessed not only in the increased interest in religious leadership, but also in the attention drawn to the inherently theological concerns embedded in organizational studies.[21] In this regard, Dyck notes how religion can contribute to management research without any general acceptance of its truth claims.[22] First, the fact that someone experiences God as a living phenomenon makes it worthy to study independent of the researcher's personal beliefs. Second, there are reasons for the sake of theory development to assume that there is a loving God, even if all agreed that no such being existed: "The theological turn enables humankind to conceive of, imagine, and theorize about concepts like altruism and genuine benefaction, concepts that have proven difficult to conceive within the conventional instrumental

18. Johns, "Adolescence of Pentecostalism," 9.

19. Warrington, *Pentecostal Theology*, 324.

20. Hamel, "Moon Shots for Management," 93.

21. Dyck and Wiebe, "Organizational Practices," 300.

22. See Dyck, "God in Management."

management paradigm."[23] Studies of religious beliefs or phenomena may introduce concepts that fall outside contemporary management models, and studies of religious leadership such as the present may, therefore, contribute a richer understanding of organizing and management beyond its immediate context.

It would be premature to solve at the outset of the study the enigma that drives the entire project: what is Pentecostal leadership, and how is such leadership experienced by leaders in the movement? Although no definition is possible or desirable at this point, there remains a need to identify the phenomenon under investigation. A leading historian of American Pentecostalism, Grant Wacker, concludes that leadership was essential to the Pentecostal movement from its very beginning—"the evidence makes clear that strong, determined, clear-eyed leaders orchestrated the revival from first to last."[24] As in every social movement, influence was—and is—asymmetrically and unevenly distributed between the revivalists. What is not clear, however, is what constitutes the inner nature of such leadership. Studies of leadership in Pentecostalism are arguably especially promising as they take place in the intersections between human (dis)ability and spiritual empowerment and the rise of charisma and the elevation of the marginalized. It is powerful leadership worked out by the socioeconomic powerless. It is leadership claimed on a basis of divine endowment, yet ending every so often in human disaster. It is leadership exercised over and with millions of people around the globe, yet its dynamics of power and influence have largely taken place below the scholarly radar.

What is called for, then, is a description of the essential structure of Pentecostal leadership. As this study attempts to answer that call, it falls into two distinct, yet related, parts. In the first part of the book, the study of Pentecostal leadership is seen from the perspective of organization and religious leadership research. This is done to locate the study within a larger field of study, to take stock of the current understanding of the phenomenon by reviewing and categorizing the extant research literature on the topic, and to set the stage for the empirical phenomenological inquiry presented in Part 2. This second main segment of the book represents the most groundbreaking features of the work, and thus deserves a more thorough introduction and explanation. While procedural details are left for chapter

23. Dyck, "God in Management," 27.
24. Wacker, *Heaven Below*, 141.

4, the following section will briefly sketch out the present research agenda and its accompanying methodology.

Toward a Phenomenology of Pentecostal Leadership

As alluded above, the overall research agenda of this book is to address the question of the meaning of Pentecostal leadership through the experiences of pastors in the movement, with the purpose of describing essential features of Pentecostal leadership in a general structure of the phenomenon. This meaning-oriented research question, combined with the relative ignorance of what characterizes leadership in Pentecostalism, calls for qualitative research strategy. It is generally accepted that exploratory qualitative studies are the better approach in areas where there is little prior research available.[25] Further, Conger argues for the prominence of qualitative strategies at all stages of leadership investigations due to the complexity of the phenomenon itself.[26] This has not always been the case in leadership research, however, as positivist paradigms have dominated the field until fairly recently.[27] Yet, if leadership essentially is about the management of meaning,[28] it is dubious that experiments and quantitative methods alone are sufficient to explain it. In Meindl's words, "Much of the trouble with conventional leadership research is attributable to the conceptual difficulties encountered when theorists and research scientists attempt to impose outside, objective, third-party definitions of what is inherently subjective."[29] This is arguably especially troublesome in studies on Pentecostalism, due to its highly flexible and diverse manifestations. Phenomenology, on the other hand, is an ideal framework for studying how people experience something because it aims at describing the essential meaning of a phenomenon in terms of subjective lived experience, hence "overcoming the strait-jacket of encrusted traditions"[30] by seeing leadership through the eyes of those who experience it. The foundational question asked in phenomenological inquiry is that of meaning, structure, and essence of the lived experience of this phenomenon for a person or group, and aims for a deeper and fuller

25. Creswell, *Research Design*, 18.
26. Conger, "Qualitative Research," 108–9.
27. Avolio et al., "Leadership," 442.
28. Smircich and Morgan, "Leadership."
29. Meindl, "Follower-Centric Theory," 339.
30. Moran, *Introduction to Phenomenology*, 4.

understanding of what it is like for someone to experience something—in this study, leadership in Pentecostal churches.

More than thirty years after Sanders' optimistic exclamation about phenomenology as "a new star on the [organizational] research horizon,"[31] one may conclude that it indeed has been a slow-rising star. While phenomenology is a frequent companion in health and education research, the approach is still to reach its peak in leadership studies. Yet, a host of authors keep arguing that qualitative studies in general,[32] and phenomenological research in particular,[33] should play a more pivotal role in leadership and management studies. Since phenomenology approaches phenomena holistically in search for their invariant meanings, it has potential to augment and expand the present knowledge on leadership by studying the lived experience of leaders. By understanding leaders' meaning and sense-making, phenomenological inquiry can "lead to startling new insights into the uniquely complex processes of . . . managing and leading."[34] In this way, phenomenology contributes to organizational research by presenting a fresh way of seeing what is discoverable and potentially there, but often ignored.[35]

For the present research agenda, phenomenology is the perfect methodological match because it holds the potential to reveal and describe the essence of lived experience and, consequently, to understand leadership as a process involving deep human dimensions. The focus is less on what actually happens in a leadership situation than it is on the lived meaning of the experience of those involved in Pentecostal leadership. As such, the starting point of inquiry is the lived experience of the phenomenon. Only by expressing it and making it articulate can its meaning emerge. This is particularly important in studies of Pentecostalism, as Pentecostals begin with rituals, affective worship, and lived experiences rather than theological thinking.[36]

The phenomenological study that makes up the backbone of this work addresses Pentecostal leadership through the experiences of Norwegian Pentecostal leadership with at least five years in the pastorate. This makes

31. Sanders, "Phenomenology," 353.

32. Alvesson and Spicer, *Metaphors We Lead By*; Klenke, *Qualitative Research*.

33. Ehrich, "Revisiting Phenomenology," 1–13; Gibson and Hanes, "Contribution of Phenomenology"; Sanders, "Phenomenology."

34. Van der Mescht, "Phenomenology in Education," 1.

35. Sanders, "Phenomenology," 357.

36. Myers, "Progressive Pentecostalism," 116.

it one *phenomenology* of Pentecostal leadership, since data collected elsewhere might have produced different results. However, the fact that context is too crucial to make universal claims does not hinder the phenomenological researcher from suggesting that findings have implications beyond the idiosyncratic and empirical. As stated above, the goal of this phenomenological project is to describe the essence of Pentecostal leadership. "Essence" here is not the same as a definition, but "a careful description of the structure of the lived experience of that phenomenon in a particular type of situation"[37]—the most invariant meaning of a phenomenon without which it cannot present itself.[38] It is thus the phenomenon itself, not the subjective experience of participants, that is the focus of the phenomenological investigation. As discussed more carefully in Part 2, the empirical descriptions are only one part of the larger data analysis, which is based on free imaginative variation (i.e., the reflective process through which one discovers which aspects of a phenomenon are essential and which are incidental) to discover the essence of the phenomenon. In Part 2, this leads to a general statement that reflects the essential structure and meaning of the lived experience of Pentecostal leadership. Consequently, it is a *phenomenology* of Pentecostal leadership, not simply a collection of individual narratives.

In short, the goal of the book is to understand the phenomenon, not to produce any grand theory of Pentecostal leadership. The latter is hardly possible for leadership in general, given its contextual and situated character. Add to that the heterogeneous nature of Pentecostalism, and the result is a highly doubtful and likely futile research agenda. The purpose of a phenomenology of Pentecostal leadership, then, is not to translate or reduce its complexity into clearly defined concepts to dispel its mystery, but rather to bring the mystery more present. To do so, the journey begins by recapitulating what is already known about the phenomenon under investigation, and is addressed in Part 1. Readers who are mostly interested in the results of the phenomenological inquiry into the meaning of Pentecostal leadership may skip this review of the extant literature and jump to the second half of the book. Although the first section of Part 2 (chapter 4) may feel a bit tedious and technical with its discussions of phenomenological philosophy and methodology—especially from a practical and pragmatic Pentecostal point of view!—I strongly recommend reading through the chapter to get an understanding of what the study seeks to do and how

37. Giorgi, "Concerning a Serious Misunderstanding," 41.
38. Giorgi, "Theory, Practice, and Evaluation," 242.

one should understand its results. In chapter 5, I describe and flesh out the essential structure of Pentecostal leadership with its empirical variations drawn from the experiences of the Norwegian pastors participating in the study. This section, together with the discussions and implications in chapters 6–7, is the main contribution of the work and provides, I believe, a broader understanding of Pentecostal leadership and a fruitful starting point for further studies of the phenomenon.

PART 1

PENTECOSTALISM AND THE STUDY OF RELIGIOUS LEADERSHIP

1

Religion in Organization and Leadership Research

BERNARD BASS NOTES THAT the interest in leadership is as old as the emergence of civilization, and that religious characters and texts represent some of the earliest examples of leaders and leadership in history.[1] While early accounts of religious leadership served a different agenda and provided answers to other questions than those posed by modern science, the study of religion and spirituality in relation to leadership is now emerging as a fruitful and interdisciplinary field attracting interest from theologians, social scientists, and organizational researchers alike. In an attempt to systematize this research, including the present study, and its relationship with the wider leadership discourse, the extant literature is divided into two groups: (a) study of religion and/or spirituality in secular organizations and theories, and (b) study of leadership in religious organizations. While the two overlap, studies in the first category primarily address how religious beliefs and spirituality lead to a special understanding of leadership and/or enrich the leadership conversation. The second category centers on normative studies of leadership in religious texts or descriptive accounts of leadership in religions or religious organizations. Studies on Pentecostal leadership belong to this second category, yet the treatise on religious leadership in secular organizations is addressed first in order to position the present work within the larger field of study.

1. Bass, *Bass Handbook of Leadership*, 4.

Religion and Spirituality in Secular Organizations

Contrary to the gloomy predictions of the secularization thesis (i.e., modernization leads to a decline of religion) dominant in the mid-twentieth century,[2] religion did not vaporize as modernity reached its zenith. With the exception of Western Europe,[3] the world today "is as furiously religious as it ever was."[4] Organization and leadership scholars have been slow to realize this trend, however. Until recently, most management theorists did not address the role of spirituality or religion, and as late as 2014 this relative ignorance sparked a volume on religion and organizational theory in Emarald's series *Research on the Sociology of Organizations*.[5] These authors suggest that the belief in the myth of declining religious importance in itself served as a barrier for studies on religion in organization and management theory.[6] Further, they highlight how the view of religion as a private affair hindered such research. As an unfortunate consequence, the concern for religion as a social force largely escaped scholarly attention. In a similar vein, Hicks believes that the neglect stems from the assumption that public organizations are secular, and thus have followed the agenda in the social sciences to model a rationality free from the trappings of religion.[7]

The tide has turned, however. At the dawn of the new millennium, hundreds of books and articles on workplace spirituality were appearing,[8] and a few years later Aburdene declared, "The quest for spirituality is the greatest megatrend of our era."[9] Zsolnai even claims that spirituality is one of the hottest emerging fields in management,[10] a statement supported by the fact that the Academy of Management has created an interest group, *Management, Spirituality, and Religion*, with several hundred members. Oswick's detection of 3,257 journal articles on spirituality recorded on the Social Sciences Citation Index database since 1970 also illustrates this

---

2. Berger, *Sacred Canopy*.
3. Davie, *Europe*.
4. Berger, *Desecularization*, 2.
5. Tracey et al., *Religion and Organization Theory*.
6. Tracey et al., "Taking Religion Seriously."
7. Hicks, "Spiritual and Religious Diversity," 380.
8. Strack and Fottler, "Spirituality and Effective Leadership," 4.
9. Aburdene, *Megatrends 2010*, 4.
10. Zsolnai, *Spirituality and Ethics*, vii.

spiritual turn in organizational research.[11] The magnitude of this development leads some authors to affirm that an average academic runs "into more spirits than Scrooge saw in a single evening."[12] Although leading journals in organizational behavior, theory, and strategy lag behind in addressing religion and spirituality,[13] it seems safe to conclude that these issues now have been firmly established on the research agenda.

One probable reason for the current interest is the reorganization of human life in modern societies, where organizations turned into major devices for coping with the problems of economic, social, and psychological change.[14] People are struggling with what spirituality means for their work as a part of their spiritual journey,[15] and the current attention given to spirituality in leadership thinking thus reflects the increased importance of work in modern societies.[16] Because the workplace has become the center of many people's lives, it is also the place where they contribute and find meaning, making it hard to separate work from the rest of their life. Another reason for the emergence of research on workplace spirituality comes from the limitations of traditional research paradigms—in particular, its rationalist approach that largely ignores the role of spirituality in organizational behavior.[17]

A critical problem in the current state of research on spirituality in organizations and leadership is the lack of clear definitions on the constructs.[18] Hicks notes that many leadership scholars define spirituality by way of negatives—spirituality is not religion.[19] Religion is typically de-

---

11. Oswick, "Burgeoning Workplace Spirituality," 17. See also Drive, "Spiritual Turn."

12. English et al., cited in Crossman, "Conceptualising Spiritual Leadership," 597.

13. Tracey, "Religion and Organization."

14. Johnson, *Ethical Challenges*, 135; Levinson, "Reciprocation."

15. Fry, "Toward a Theory."

16. Fairholm, "Spiritual Leadership."

17. Crossman, "Conceptualising Spiritual Leadership," 598–99; Nicolae et al., "Where Do We Stand," 557.

18. Benefiel, "Second Half"; Strack and Fottler, "Spirituality and Effective Leadership," 9.

19. Hicks, "Spiritual and Religious Diversity." Symptomatically, it is estimated that less than 20 percent of the literature on workplace spirituality refers to a deity (Dyck, "God in Management," 53). Hicks is critical of this religion/spirituality dichotomy, and feels that proponents of workplace spirituality fail in their emphasis on bringing the whole person to work if their spirituality are robbed from any religious content and meaning. Rather than suppressing religion from the marketplace, Hicks proposes a leadership framework in which conflicting perspectives—also religious—can be negotiated in the organization.

scribed as rigid and dogmatic, while spirituality is about meaning, transcendence, growth, and harmony—the former divisive and partisan, the latter unifying and holistic.

> Spirituality is the privatization of religion, informal, personal, universal, nondenominational, inclusive, tolerant, positive, individualistic, less visible and quantifiable, subjective, emotionally oriented and inwardly directed, less authoritarian, little external accountability, and appropriate to be expressed in the workplace.[20]

Dent, Higgins, and Wharff note that this distinction between religion and spirituality is a major point of disagreement in the discourse on spiritual leadership.[21] Strack and Fottler contend, "Spirituality is a complex, abstract, and multidimensional concept that has no consensus on definition among leading scholars."[22] This lack of clear definition and conceptualization continues to be a major weakness of the field.[23]

However, this conceptual ambiguity has not hindered the development of spiritual leadership as a field within the broader context of workplace spirituality. Spiritual leadership is described from different vantage points and in various contexts—for instance, in the military,[24] in education,[25] in church,[26] and in health care.[27] This development of spiritual leadership is typically seen as part of an increased emphasis on ethics in leadership.[28]

In addition to proposals of distinct theories of spiritual leadership,[29] researchers have addressed how religious beliefs and constructs may inform organizational research. One example is calling, where the literature has burgeoned in social sciences over the last few years.[30] The notion of a

20. Liu and Robertson, "Spirituality in the Workplace," 35.

21. Dent et al., "Spirituality and Leadership."

22. Strack and Fottler, "Spirituality and Effective Leadership," 8.

23. Liu and Robertson, "Spirituality in the Workplace"; Nicolae et al., "Where Do We Stand," 35.

24. Fry et al., "Impact of Spiritual Leadership"; Fry et al., "Spiritual Leadership."

25. Karadağ, "Spiritual Leadership"; Nooralizad et al., "Casual Model."

26. Murray and Evers, "Reweaving the Fabric"; Statnick, "Elements of Spiritual Leadership."

27. Dent et al., "Spirituality and Leadership."

28. Bass, *Bass Handbook of Leadership*, 213; Johnson, *Ethical Challenges*, 136–40; Yukl, *Leadership in Organizations*, 338–39.

29. E.g., Fairholm, "Spiritual Leadership"; Fry, "Toward a Theory."

30. Duffy and Dik, "Research on Calling."

calling has traditionally been associated with religion, but recent streams of organizational research claim that religious beliefs or orientation are neither necessary nor sufficient to have a calling.[31] On the contrary, researchers frequently use the term "calling" to describe people's attitude and fulfillment in the workplace regardless, of spiritual orientation or religious affiliation.

Spirituality is also connected to management more subtly in approaches such as servant leadership and transformational leadership. Not only are central tenets of spiritual leadership models derived from these other constructs;[32] spirituality is also evident in transformational and servant leadership theories.[33] For instance, Sendjaya, Sarros, and Santora discuss spiritual leadership, servant leadership, authentic leadership, and transformational leadership under the heading of value-laden research, and suggest that spirituality is especially important for the first two constructs.[34] These authors note how servant and spiritual leadership both seek to facilitate intrinsically motivating work environment and argue that spiritual leadership is embedded in servant leadership. The question of whether the different constructs are distinct or describe the same underlying variable is peripheral to the present discussion. What the brief review attempts to reveal is rather the impact of and interest in spirituality in contemporary leadership research.

Leadership in Religious Organizations

The second category of religion and spirituality in leadership centers on leadership in religious organization. This research stream is by no means restricted to Christian organizations. Since Pentecostalism belongs to the Christian religion, however, the present work is primarily interested in studies on Christian leadership.

McClymond note the striking lack of interest in religious leadership among scholars in the twentieth century.[35] According to Lindt, this limited

31. E.g., Duffy et al., "Perceiving a Calling"; Hall and Chandler, "Psychological Success"; Steger et al., "Calling in Work."

32. Nicolae et al., "Where Do We Stand," 554.

33. Crossman, "Conceptualising Spiritual Leadership," 600–603; Fernando, "Spirituality and Leadership," 485–86.

34. Sendjaya et al., "Servant Leadership Behavior."

35. McClymond, "Prophet or Loss?"

attention to leadership in the scientific study of religion has resulted in little advancement beyond Max Weber and Joachim Wach's initial studies in the area.[36] Recently, however, the turn to spirituality and theology in management research discussed above has been paralleled by an increased interest in religious leadership, especially Christian and biblical perspectives on leadership.[37] This trend is witnessed by the growing number of academic journals addressing religious leadership (e.g., *Journal of Management, Spirituality & Religion, Journal of Religious Leadership, Journal of Biblical Perspectives in Leadership, Journal of Applied Christian Leadership,* and *Scandinavian Journal of Leadership and Theology*) and the inclusion of theologically informed articles in mainstream leadership publications.[38]

One probable reason for the current interest in leadership in evangelical and Pentecostal circles is the church growth movement's attempt to "integrate the eternal theological principles from God's word . . . with the best insights of contemporary social and behavioral sciences."[39] This paradigm—together with the notion of an apostolic revolution in many Pentecostal churches[40]—has led to an increased emphasis on strong, visionary, and entrepreneurial leadership.[41] Together with the prominence of the megachurch, this highlighting of leadership and management is arguably the result of an emphasis on pragmatic and practical intelligence in church growth strategy.[42] Whether this interest in leadership represents a break away from bureaucratic thinking and operational Great Man theories of leadership remains an open question. Given the Weberian notion that Protestant work ethics underpin conventional management theories, one should not be surprised if Bible-oriented researchers argue that mainstream management models are consistent with Christian values.[43]

According to Dyck, religious scriptures are the main source of religious influence on management literature.[44] His research reveals that about 80 percent of the articles on religion and management in organization and leadership journals deal with holy texts, with the remaining 20 percent

36. Lindt, "Leadership," 5383.

37. Bekker, "Towards a Theoretical Model," 142–43.

38. E.g., Whittington et al., "Legacy Leadership."

39. Rainer, *Book of Church Growth*, 19–20.

40. Cartledge, *Apostolic Revolution*; Wagner, *Churchquake.*

41. See Åkerlund, "Pentekostale Former."

42. Clifton, *Pentecostal Churches in Transition,* chap. 4.

43. Dyck, "God in Management," 35.

44. Dyck, "God in Management," 30.

talking about the effects of religious practices (prayer, meditation, mindfulness, etc.). The reference to religious texts in management writings does not point in one direction, however. Regarding the Bible, Dyck shows that it has been used to support both conventional and radical management theory. The former typically follows Weber's ideas on Protestant work ethics, and argues in favor of the free-market system and mainstream management literature and practice. In contrast, the radical approach argues for a more countercultural understanding of business and management, with less emphasis on profit, materialism, and individualism. Dyck concludes that religious scriptures are interpreted in opposite ways with regard to their implications for management:

> About half of the studies interpret religious scriptures to provide support for enhancing mainstream management, and the other half interpret scriptures to call for a liberating radical approach to management. These divergent implications of scriptures for management may suggest that the scriptures are ambiguous or unclear, that people have not studied them carefully enough, or that people are clever enough to interpret them to say whatever they want to hear.[45]

The final clause corresponds with what Kessler describes as a pitfall in biblical leadership, namely the ignorance of cultural influence on any attempt to construct a purely scriptural leadership theory and the assimilation of secular leadership theories in such an endeavor.[46] As an antidote, Dyck proposes that scholars working with management from a scriptural vantage point should pay more attention to the understanding of management at the time in which these scriptures were originally written. If the historical context was brought into analyses with the same rigor given to other research questions, Dyck believes that the scholarly community would speak with a more unified voice than is the case today.

While certainly a much welcome proposal, the critique against lacking historical rigor in studies on scriptural leadership arguably misses the mark regarding the growing stream of research addressing religious and Christian leadership. There are, of course, examples of what Kessler perceives to be a fallacy of reconstruction—that is, the reading of contemporary leadership theories into the biblical texts. For instance, Kessler suggests that the contemporary accentuation of visionary leadership in Christian

---

45. Dyck, "God in Management," 52.
46. Kessler, "Pitfalls in 'Biblical' Leadership."

circles reflects this misconception.[47] In a similar vein, Åkerlund argues that the presentations of servant leadership as the prime model of Christian leadership fail to reflect the various meanings of servanthood in the Bible.[48] Niewold takes it a step further and accuses servant leadership theory of promoting a heterodox Christology.[49]

However, an important trend in research on leadership within biblical studies over the last decades is the use of social–historical frameworks to understand the cultural world behind the text and the narrative world within the text. Such use of theories from the social sciences have produced original studies on the dynamics of power of leadership within the early church.[50] Particularly important in this regard is Andrew Clarke's research on Pauline leadership. Through three monographs on leadership in the Pauline corpus, Clarke has emerged as one of the prominent New Testament scholars in the emerging field of Christian leadership. While Clarke's first study primarily dealt with leadership in Corinth,[51] he has later sought to compare leadership across the Pauline churches and their Greco-Roman contexts.[52] More recently, Clarke has provided a generic and systematic study of leadership in the Pauline corpus.[53]

At this stage, the growing body of research on biblical and Christian leadership is multifaceted both in content and methodology. Bekker suggests that the recent interest in Christian leadership has been characterized by (a) studies of leadership approaches of biblical characters; (b) historical, sociological, and contextual descriptions; (c) studies of historical Christian figures; (d) ethical explorations; (e) cross-faith comparative analysis; (f) formational process descriptions; (g) comparisons with leadership and management theories; (h) exegetical studies; and (i) attempts at a proto-theory.[54] The present work seeks to provide a unique contribution to the understanding of leadership in religious organizations by exploring Pentecostal leadership. In order to understand the phenomenon, then, the religious context in which it plays out must be addressed.

47. Kessler, "Pitfalls in 'Biblical' Leadership," 4–6.

48. Åkerlund, "Son, Sent, and Servant."

49. Niewold, "Beyond Servant Leadership."

50. E.g., Åkerlund, "Leadership in Corinth"; Barentsen, *Emerging Leadership*; Chow, *Patronage and Power*; Holmberg, *Paul and Power*; Tucker, *You Belong to Christ*.

51. Clarke, *Secular and Christian Leadership*.

52. Clarke, *Serve the Community*.

53. Clarke, *Pauline Theology*.

54. Bekker, "Towards a Theoretical Model."

2

Understanding Pentecostalism

No successful metatheory of the origins of the worldwide Pentecostal movement exists, and discussions on the historiography of the movement within the United States and on the global scene reveal a variety of understandings of the phenomenon and its proper research methodology. It is outside the scope of this study to engage the discussion in any detail. It suffices to say that, while the present work follows what Robeck described as the dominant storyline in historical research on the globalization of Pentecostalism,[1] starting with Seymour and the Azusa Street revival in 1906, it acknowledges that not everyone shares this accentuation of its American roots.[2] For the initiation of the Norwegian Pentecostal movement, however, the impetus from the Azusa Street revival is indisputable and explains the emphasis on this line of development.

1. Robeck, "Origins of Modern Pentecostalism," 20.

2. Anderson claims that academic studies on Pentecostalism have been misinformed by a North-American and European bias that has downplayed the importance of movements emanating from outside the US. Rather than reckoning Azusa Street as the epicenter of Pentecostalism, it is hence probably more correct to see this revival as part of a wider series of outpourings that had equal significance in the global spread of the early Pentecostal movement (Anderson, *Spreading Fires*, 290–91). See also Anderson, *Introduction to Pentecostalism*; Hollenweger, *Pentecostalism*; and Synan, *Holiness-Pentecostal Tradition* for various perspectives on the historical roots of the Pentecostal movement.

Globalization

From the humble beginnings in Azusa Street, Pentecostalism became the most dynamic and fastest growing segment of church in the twentieth century, and is likely to become the dominant form of Christianity in the twenty-first century.[3] Observers have reported an estimated 700 percent increase in Pentecostal believers over the last three decades, making up a quarter of the world's Christian population and two-thirds of all Protestants.[4] Though counting such a diverse movement is a complex task, recent statistics report more than 640 million Pentecostals worldwide in 2015, with numbers expected to hover around 1.1 billion by 2050.[5]

Miller and Yamamori suggest that Pentecostalism is the engine behind the massive changes in world Christianity over the last hundred years—including the shift from the Global North to the Global South, the growth of Protestantism and the decline of Catholicism in South America, the sway away from liturgical forms to vibrant worship, and the expansion of independent churches amidst the decline of mainline denominations.[6] The movement's ability to cross over social, cultural, and geographical borders has been described in the literature for some decades now, reflected in Cox's portrayal of "a religion made to travel"[7] and Martin's assertion that the world is their parish.[8] It is hence common for observers of the expansion of Pentecostalism to treat the movement as an integral part of the globalization process as well as a product of it.[9] Though dissonance remains as to how globalization should be understood and conceptualized in Pentecostal scholarship,[10] there is no doubt that Pentecostalism is a global phenomenon and has been so from its beginning—"it is truly the first global religion."[11] As such, migration and mission work are two important themes in Pentecostal studies.

---

3. Casanova, "Religion, the New Millennium," 435.

4. Anderson et al., *Studying Global Pentecostalism*, 2.

5. Johnson et al., "Christianity 2015."

6. Miller and Yamamori, *Global Pentecostalism*.

7. Cox, *Fire from Heaven*, 102.

8. Martin, *Pentecostalism*.

9. Deininger, *Global Pentecostalism*.

10. Wilkinson, "What's 'Global' about Global Pentecostalism," 96–97.

11. Casanova, "Religion, the New Millennium," 437.

Pentecostalism has shown a remarkable ability to adapt to diverse cultural contexts. Through its adaptability, its impact has been global, both in its geographic distribution and in its presence as a religious movement capable of producing local versions of its universal message.[12]

Wilkinson rightly points out that Pentecostalism does not merely spread around the world; it also changes in the process.[13] Hence, one must account for its transformation and how it both shapes and is shaped by sociocultural forces in its context. Though this reciprocal process is not the main interest in this study, one needs to be aware of the differing settings in which Pentecostalism exists and how these have influenced the movement, including the plethora of forms and expressions of Pentecostal spirituality and leadership. In a paradoxical manner, Pentecostalism is able to engage local contexts while at the same time establishing its own cultural frameworks, hence rejecting and preserving the cultures it encounters.[14]

The inherent fluidity of Pentecostalism has made it the quintessential "glocalized" religion by transcending the local and propagating "a universal 'imaginary of the world,' while at the same time incorporating itself successfully into the sociocultural contexts of any new cultures it encounters."[15] The cultural dimensions of globalized Pentecostalism may thus be summarized in its ability to act in different and opposite ways at once, meaning that the observable contradictions and paradoxes are essential and foundational to the movement. This inherent diversity of Pentecostalism has led some authors to suggest that one should probably speak of "Pentecostalisms" in plural with the experience of the Spirit as a unifying element that brings people together and transcends differences.[16]

Characteristics and Definitions

While the previous section serves as a backdrop of the present study by providing insights into the history and current situation of worldwide Pentecostalism, it also reveals the diverse character of the Pentecostal

12. Anderson et al., *Studying Global Pentecostalism*, 1.

13. Wilkinson, "Many Tongues," 8.

14. Robbins, "Globalization," 118–19.

15. Deininger, *Global Pentecostalism*, 92.

16. Anderson, *Introduction to Pentecostalism*, 286; Kärkkäinen, "Pentecostal Pneumatologies," 161.

movement and, consequently, the inherent problem of providing clear-cut definitions of the phenomenon. Pentecostalism is a prime example of how religion adapts in contemporary history, and the movement is so complex that it is neither possible nor helpful to use distinct categories in describing it. State Miller and Yamamori, "The problem with generalizing about Pentecostalism, however, is that it is such an unruly movement. Wherever it emerges, Pentecostalism tends to indigenize, absorbing the local culture in the way it worships, organizes itself, and relates to the local community."[17] Hence, they suggest that Pentecostalism is better described in terms of a wild shrub than a tree with symmetrical branches. It holds diversity of biblical proportions: "Like the beasts in Noah's ark, Pentecostals come in a bewildering variety," claims Wacker[18]—and I assume that his analogy stops at the movement's variety!

Ma, Kärkkäinen, and Asamoah-Gyadu suggest several problems with pinning down Pentecostalism in any monolithic fashion.[19] First, due to its short history, it cannot build on any ecclesial tradition. Second, until recently, the movement has not produced much academic literature, but rather contributed with writings and testimonies that hardly match the categories of analytic scholarship. Third, Pentecostalism has incorporated elements from the various traditions from which it emerged and, therefore, poses a dynamic theology in the making. With this rather flexible and syncretistic repertoire of theology and practices, many scholars prefer to define Pentecostal identity in terms of spirituality rather than theology. Arguing from this stance, Anderson contends that any definition based on doctrine is futile because Pentecostalism favors experience over formal theology.[20] Consequently, he describes Pentecostalism as a movement concerned with the experience of the works of the Spirit and the practice of spiritual gift.

In a similar manner, Plüss argues that attention to the presence and power of Holy Spirit in life and creation is what Pentecostal churches and denominations have in common.[21] Casanova agrees and contends that Pentecostals share a focus on the gifts of the Spirit, as well as an emphasis on emotional and experiential expressions over discursive and doctrinal

---

17. Miller and Yamamori, *Global Pentecostalism*, 211.

18. Wacker, "Wild Theories and Mad Excitement," 20.

19. Ma et al., *Pentecostal Mission and Global Christianity*.

20. Anderson, *Introduction to Pentecostalism*, 14.

21. See Plüss, "Frog King."

aspects in common.[22] Likewise, Smith refrains from labeling Pentecostalism along historical or denominational lines, but defines it as "an understanding of Christian faith that is open to the continued operations of the Spirit"[23]—hence including charismatic traditions outside the classical Pentecostal denominations. This wide definition epitomizes a final problem in proposing any clear-cut definition of Pentecostalism, namely the early movements' relationship to the subsequent charismatic movements that share some, but not all, of its characteristics. It is common to describe this relationship in terms of three connected but distinct waves: (a) classical Pentecostals organized into denominations early in the twentieth century; (b) charismatic movements within traditional denominations from the 1960s; and (c) neo-charismatic/Pentecostals represented by innumerable nondenominational churches around the world. While this taxonomy is widely held, the debate about the contours of three groups of Pentecostalism is not settled.[24] For the present study, however, the Norwegian Pentecostal movement belongs to this first category.

Despite the diversity within its ranks, Anderson et al. identified five typifying characteristics of global Pentecostalism.[25] First, the movement has given a new form to the Christian message by emphasizing the role and gifts of the Holy Spirit. Second, it has experienced a surprising numerical growth and, hence, proved the secularization thesis wrong for most parts of the world. Third, Pentecostalism is flexible in the way that it adapts to heterogeneous settings while remaining faithful to its identity. Accordingly, it has produced a myriad of manifestations, also in the area of organizing and leadership studied in this work. Fourth, the flexibility mentioned in the previous point has made the movement able to attract a variety of audiences, each of which adapts and draws from different parts of the Pentecostal repertoire. Finally, that most Pentecostals live in the Global South has fueled its fame as a special case in the field of religion. These common characteristics do not undermine the fact that Pentecostalism remains especially hard to define. The movement's internal diversity is a part of its

22. Casanova, "Religion, the New Millennium," 435.

23. Smith, *Thinking in Tongues*, loc. 200.

24. Laan, "Historical Approaches," 204–5; Ma et al., *Pentecostal Mission and Global Christianity*, 20:3–4.

25. Anderson et al., *Studying Global Pentecostalism*, 3.

self-description, and any attempt to nail down a fixed understanding of Pentecostal identity is doomed to fail.[26] According to Währisch-Oblau,

> Pentecostalism is a movement without clear borders, and its identities will be defined differently by different people in different contexts, and are constantly being negotiated and re-negotiated within the movement. Identities are constructed and reconstructed according to the need of delimiting one's own against "the other."[27]

This problem is solved in the current study by defining the phenomenon organizationally, narrowing it down to leaders in the Norwegian Pentecostal movement. Although other churches and denominations in Norway certainly belong to the wide and inclusive description of Pentecostalism used by Anderson and others, the present work draws attention to leadership as it is experienced by pastors in the denomination, originating from the revivals in Oslo early in the twentieth century. As such, a brief introduction of the Norwegian Pentecostal movement is necessary.

The Norwegian Pentecostal Movement

Pentecostalism in Norway has long been under scholarly scrutiny. Bloch-Hoell's doctoral dissertation on the Norwegian Pentecostal movement was among the first academic studies of Pentecostalism,[28] and numerous scholarly works have discussed various aspects of Pentecostalism in Norway.[29] Although Norwegian Pentecostalism is larger than one man, the movement is inseparably connected with the life and ministry of Thomas Ball Barratt, "the founder and prime motivator of early Pentecostalism in Europe."[30]

Barratt was born in England in 1862, but moved to Norway when he was four because his father started as the manager of a mine in the country. Young Thomas felt a deeper drawing to God from early years and started to preach when he was sixteen years old. In 1885, Thomas quit his musical studies with the famous Norwegian composer Edvard Grieg to become a Methodist preacher, and later moved to Oslo (former Christiania), where

26. Deininger, *Global Pentecostalism*, 37.

27. Währisch-Oblau, *Missionary Self-Perception*, 45.

28. Bloch-Hoell, *Pinsebevegelsen*.

29. E.g., Alvarsson, "Scandinavian Countries"; Bundy, "Historical and Theological Analysis"; Bundy, *Visions of Apostolic Mission*; Tangen, "Pentecostal Movements in Norway."

30. Anderson, *To the Ends of the Earth*, 55.

he founded the Christiania City Mission, an interdenominational society in the city. This work expanded to such an extent that they had to build a center, and in September 1905, Barratt left for America to raise funds for the new building. The fundraising came to be a great disappointment, as the meetings in major US cities did not bring the money Barratt had hoped for, and he planned to return to Norway in June 1906. Two Methodist bishops urged him to stay for some more months, and during this time Barratt read about the revival in Azusa Street, Los Angeles. After weeks of prayer and longing for the phenomenon reported from California, he experienced what he described as a baptism in the Holy Spirit on November 15.

Barratt started Pentecostal meetings when returning to Norway in December 1906, and his own newspaper *Byposten* soon reported that the revival had broken out in Christiania. The Pentecostal Movement was soon front-page news in the Norwegian daily press. The revival spread remarkably fast and, in 1907, the Pentecostal Movement spread to at least fifty-one different places in Norway.[31] Barratt established a Pentecostal assembly in Oslo in 1916, and between 1927 and 1933, an average of over one Pentecostal congregation was organized monthly in Norway.[32] Barratt emerged as a key leader on the domestic and international scene, with the revival in Oslo as the one main center for Pentecostalism in Europe.[33]

While revivalism continued to impact parts of the movement after Barratt's death in 1940, the following decades may well be described under headings such as consolidating institutionalization, charismatic renewal, and conflicts.[34] In terms of the latter, the exclusion of the entrepreneurial evangelist Aril Edvardsen led to a rift within the movement between traditional Pentecostals and more progressive leaders. While the movement was relatively homogeneous up until this point, Maurset contends that the expulsion of Edvardsen marked a shift toward more openness and diversity in the movement, and traces fundamental changes in the movement since then:[35] (a) countercultural aspects were downplayed, including the former accentuation of holiness and righteous living; (b) a homogeneous fundamentalist hermeneutic was replaced with more diversity in theology and expressions; (c) an active focus on engaging, loving, and impacting the

---

31. Bloch-Hoell, *Pentecostal Movement*, 68.
32. Bloch-Hoell, *Pentecostal Movement*, 73.
33. Kay, "Sociological Perspective," 387.
34. Tangen, "Pentecostal Movements in Norway," 201–5.
35. Maurset, "Frå Helgingsrørsle til Marknadsrørsle."

world had subdued the escapist impulse to flee an evil world; and (d) char-ismatic utterances were less visible in public gatherings, and eschatological preaching was almost nonexistent. However, Maurset notes that pockets of the movement have preserved the more traditional forms, especially in rural areas. The first years of the new millennium were also marked by increased ecumenism and church planting.[36] The Norwegian Pentecostal movement currently consists of approximately three hundred congrega-tions across the country, with a total of forty thousand members.

36. Tangen, "Pentecostal Movements in Norway," 205–6.

3

Present Understandings of
Pentecostal Leadership

IN THE PREVIOUS CHAPTERS, I provided the conceptual and contextual background for the study of Pentecostal leadership. With this in mind, the study now turns to the extant literature on Pentecostal leadership. What follows is an extensive, but by no means complete, inventory of what is written on the topic, and an attempt to highlight, thematize, and discuss important aspects and characteristics of leadership in the Pentecostal movement. Without framing the character of the phenomenon prior to data analysis, the following sections chart the territory of Pentecostal leadership to set the stage for the subsequent phenomenological inquiry into the meaning of leadership in this particular ecclesial context. As such, they provide a link between the present state and what is lacking in our understanding of leadership in Pentecostalism, reinforcing the need and rationale for the present research agenda. In organizing the material, I have summarized the literature under three headings—Called and Empowered, Diverse and Contextual, and Charismatic and Enigmatically Powerful. Although heuristic, these categories have emerged from my reading of the literature, and as such represent an effort to elevate the level of abstraction toward a more general understanding of Pentecostal leadership.

Called and Empowered

Though literature on Pentecostal leaders abound, few attempts have been made to present a systematic treatise of Pentecostal leadership. In an article on Pentecostal leaders, Christel warns against painting a picture of Pentecostal leadership with broad strokes, as there is great diversity across generations and contexts of Pentecostal leaders. She narrows the study to classic Pentecostals (US Assemblies of God) and suggested that leadership stems from being led and empowered by the Spirit, as "their leadership is grounded in a deep sense of God's calling them and giving them a mission."[1] Love and burden for the lost are what motivates these leaders, who rely on the empowering gifts of the Spirit in executing their leadership. In terms of leadership models, Christel contends that Pentecostal leaders primarily look to Jesus' example of servant leadership and try to translate this ideal into an effective leadership style in leading their congregations. They reject top-down hierarchy and rely on transformational leadership by encouraging team-based ministry and involving others in setting direction for the church. Also, they mobilize members of their congregations for compassionate work in their local communities.[2]

The literature has confirmed Christel's emphasis on the centrality of divine calling and empowerment for leaders in Pentecostalism. Radical conversion experiences are common among Pentecostal pastors,[3] and researchers have begun to explore the role of calling in Pentecostal leadership. Unlike the reformed tradition, where everyone has a calling (religious or not), calling in the Pentecostal tradition has a distinct flavor. While everyone is called to repentance and relationship with God, "Pentecostals believe that a calling is a special claim that God places on the life of the believer to

---

1. Christel, "Pentecostal Leader," 121.

2. While Christel highlights important aspects of Pentecostal ministry and leadership, there is a lack of critical distance and empirical support for the rather hagiographic descriptions of Pentecostal leaders as humble and committed people who fervently seek God in prayer, Scripture, and fasting, sacrificially pursuing a God-given vision beyond the leader's capacity. Put bluntly, the article does not provide much clarity to the phenomenon of Pentecostal leadership, but rather conflates what ideally should happen with what actually happens.

3. Gooren, "Conversion Narratives," 106–8; Miller and Yamamori, *Global Pentecostalism*, 186. Having a vision and being called is also more common among Pentecostal founders than non-profit entrepreneurs from other Christian traditions (Scheitle and Adamczyk, "Divine Callings," 109).

be in ministry and that not everyone receives one."[4] All of Währisch-Oblau's respondents (i.e., pastors from the Global South leading Pentecostal/Charismatic migrant congregations in Germany) agree and claim that, to be a real pastor, the individual has to be called directly by God.[5] Given the enormous pressure on the pastorate in European migrant congregations, Währisch-Oblau finds it hardly surprising that divine power is a central element of the leaders' self-understanding, and notes that calling and supernatural enabling are interconnected in the Pentecostal pastorate.

Although calling experiences in Pentecostalism may vary due to cultural and denominational contexts, Währisch-Oblau holds that they are valid only if they can be recounted; a person with a calling by necessity has a calling narrative. Since Pentecostalism is highly experiential and defined more by testimonies than doctrinal reflection, the telling of these narratives legitimizes the authority of the person being called; "by recounting a call testimony, pastors establish and strengthen their special position in relation to the congregation."[6]

The form and content of the calling experience is not the same, however. In a qualitative study proposing a model of calling development, Markow found that the calling of Pentecostal pastors went through five stages—awaiting, awakening, actualization, anguish, and acceptance.[7] Although the participants reported that they recognized the call through spiritual awakening or involvement, not all experienced an epiphany or manifestation (vision, sign, a word from God himself), as often is expected in Pentecostal circles. Interestingly, not all of Währisch-Oblau's respondents referred to dramatic manifestations either. Währisch-Oblau suspects that this diversity results from interview setting in which such elements were not necessary to legitimize their pastoral roles. In another context, the interviewees may have given a narrative including vision or dreams. The function of the story hence dictates its form. In summary, Währisch-Oblau revealed that calling narratives are used as a legitimizing device in Pentecostal groups, especially in settings where the leader is challenged or his/her authority is questioned.

4. Markow, "Calling and Leader Identity," 24.

5. Währisch-Oblau, *Missionary Self-Perception*.

6. Währisch-Oblau, *Missionary Self-Perception*, 86; Åkerlund, "When the Fire Fell"; Andersson, "To Live the Biblical Narratives."

7. Markow, "Calling and Leader Identity."

Diverse and Contextual

In a recent article on Pentecostal leadership, Åkerlund uses Wacker's distinction between the primitive and the pragmatic to describe the enigma of Pentecostal leadership's ability to combine spiritual energy and orientation, while at the same time being unabashedly flexible in earthly affairs.[8] "Primitivism" here refers to otherworldliness, the yearning to be guided by the Spirit in every aspect of life. "Pragmatism," on the other hand, refers to Pentecostalism's willingness to work with contemporary social and cultural structures. The way these seemingly incompatible impulses interplay in Pentecostalism partly explains the genius of the Pentecostal revival: "For all of their declarations about living solely in the realm of the supernatural, with the Holy Spirit guiding every step of their lives, they nonetheless displayed a remarkably clear-eyed vision of the way things worked here on earth."[9] While early Pentecostal leaders attributed their work to the Spirit, even to the degree that some of their periodicals refused to list a human editor, Wacker insists that leaders were always there assessing realities, setting direction, and implementing strategies.

The local and contextual nature of global Pentecostalism displays the interaction between primitivism and pragmatism described by Wacker. It is "the quintessential indigenous religion, adapting readily to a variety of cultures,"[10] and its pragmatism combined with an emphasis on spiritual experiences opens Pentecostalism for ideas, models, and strategies from various backgrounds.[11] A keyword here is "contextualization," that is, the idea that Christianity must adapt to particular contexts to be meaningful. This notion is by no means restricted to the global spread of Pentecostalism, as Christian missionaries of all times have struggled with the cultural consequences of the gospel. Mission history is a case study in continuity and discontinuity, of cultural transformation and enculturation on local premises. However, the expansion of the Pentecostal movement has intensified the discussion and left scholars with an intriguing paradox of more continuity and discontinuity with local contexts than is customary in mainline Christian missions.[12] Still, Pentecostalism has not been drawn into the debate

---

8. Åkerlund, "Pentekostale Former."

9. Wacker, *Heaven Below*, 13.

10. Klaus, "Pentecostalism as a Global Culture," 127.

11. Samuel, "Pentecostalism as a Global Culture."

12. Lindhardt, "Continuity, Change or Coevalness," 163–64.

about contextualization in any significant way.[13] This may stem from the fact that contextualization within Pentecostalism has been unthematized and the result of a highly practical mission strategy, rather than sustained reflection.[14] Although this approach to mission undoubtedly has proven itself to be effective, it has also been blemished with "signs and blunders."[15]

In an attempt to systematize Pentecostal contextualization practices, Lord argues that Pentecostal contextualization takes the form of translation and synthetic models.[16] The former refers to an understanding of the gospel as unchanging truth, and contexts as mere vehicles for the translation of this message into various cultures. In contrast, the synthetic model does not lock revelation into a set of propositions, but puts more emphasis on socio-cultural environments by insisting that the church converses with the context to better understand its faith and mission.[17] While the translation model epitomizes much of early Pentecostal missions, Lord contends that there has been an increasing synthetic engagement with the world that is more positive toward cultural forms and experiences and facilitates a two-way transformation of culture and church. The new strand of Progressive Pentecostalism reported by Miller and Yamamori supports this trend and highlights both adaptability and active social engagement as emergent elements of the Pentecostal movement, predominantly in the Global South.[18] This movement represents a fusion of Pentecostal worship and spirituality with grassroot efforts to provide relief, education, development, and health services.

However, the synthesis of local flavor and Pentecostal characteristics in not necessarily the result of conscious contextual theology in which (local) leaders discern the claims of the Gospel in a dialogue between Scripture, tradition, and culture. Writing from an African perspective, Lindhardt claims that religious tolerance is more the brainchild of Western and African intellectuals than the dominant view on grassroot level among African Pentecostals. Rather than looking for signs of God or Christian values in local, traditional religions, Pentecostals have with great success adapted to "the needs and concerns of many Africans, *without* making

13. Lord, *Spirit-Shaped Mission*, 92.

14. Kärkkäinen, "Culture, Contextualization, and Conversion," 274.

15. Anderson, "Signs and Blunders."

16. Lord, "Pentecostal Mission."

17. The models are taken from Bevans, *Models of Contextual Theology*.

18. Miller and Yamamori, *Global Pentecostalism*.

much conscious attempt to create a sympathetic and tolerant synthesis with existing cultures."[19] Consequently, there is simultaneously a rejection and a de facto acceptance of local ontologies. One example of this paradox is the emphasis on spiritual warfare in African Pentecostalism, where the existence and potency of traditional spirit-cosmologies remain unquestioned, while new ways of dealing with them are provided.

In a similar manner, there is evidence suggesting that, while Pentecostal leaders cannot rely on traditional hierarchies or leadership bases, they continue to function within traditional leadership structures. McCauley argues that the concept of "big man rule," originally referring to patron-client relationships based on kin, can be used to describe Pentecostal leadership in Africa.[20] He contends that Pentecostalism replaces traditional clientelism eroded by socio-economic changes in African societies (i.e., the state's failure to provide social welfare and its expanding control over customary activities, increased urbanization, and change in social values due to the global financial crisis). Together, these factors contribute to undermining traditional big man rule and open up room for other players to attain power. In this respect, McCauley suggests that Pentecostal leaders both mirror and replace traditional big man rule by encouraging members to break from their past and trust their leadership by committing exclusively to their religious social network. Thus, a social equilibrium evolves between Pentecostal leaders and their followers, but it is one that hinges on church members' embrace of the leader as a God-like figure. Consequently, the Pentecostal form of big man rule centers on "leaders who embrace their special callings to bring the Holy Spirit to worshipers. From that foundation of spiritual commitment, a patron-client form of exchange can develop in mutually beneficial fashion."[21]

What is interesting in this line of reasoning for the present study, is how seemingly intra-religious practices and concerns translate into political power. It illustrates how the architecture of Pentecostalism in Africa has given it competitive advantages, not only vis-à-vis other churches or religions, but also over secular organizations. Pentecostalism creates new reciprocal structures that replicate the exchange of resources for loyalty central to conventional big man rule, yet in another key. By including miracles and spiritual goods into the exchange, "Pentecostal big men compensate loyalty

19. Lindhardt, "Introduction," 13.
20. McCauley, "Africa's New Big Man Rule?"
21. McCauley, "Pentecostals and Politics," 324.

not only with tangible resources, but also with the psychological benefits of promised blessings."[22] Ironically, then, the lack of traditional powerbases and hierarchy turns out to be beneficial, since Pentecostal leaders are free to target follower needs and to challenge established patrons in ways that mainline religious leaders cannot do.[23]

In short, Pentecostal leaders fill a void created by ineffective state organizations and socio-cultural currents, and provide new social networks in turbulent times. In doing so, Pentecostal leadership both continues and transforms traditional African power-structures. As interesting as it may be, it is outside the scope of this work to address Pentecostalism's influence on political leadership in any length.[24] It is the ecclesial and organizational aspects of Pentecostal leadership that is center stage in this work. Still, these developments show how the Pentecostal movement and its leaders both adapt to and alter the social forces and structures at work in the culture that they inhabit. In Robbin's words, "it preserves that which it breaks from" by addressing peoples' concerns about the spiritual world while altering the moral value of these beliefs.[25] In doing so, Pentecostal leaders attach their message to locally meaningful idioms in explaining the past, present, and future. While the evils they attack vary from setting to setting, the dualism between the divine and the demonic is relatively stable across contexts.[26] Casanova notes the paradox: "It is in their very struggle against local culture that they prove how locally rooted they are."[27]

That Pentecostal leadership is inherently prone to contextualization is further witnessed in its willingness to address worldly problems and the emphasis on self-supporting, self-propagating, and self-governing churches in Pentecostal missions. Robbins points to the fact that Pentecostal mission churches tend to be governed by locals, staffed from the bottom with natives who are responsive to local situations.[28] He contends that this inclination to build and maintain institutions inexpensively and contextually stems from the belief that it is the Spirit's power that makes the difference, not educa-

---

22. McCauley, "Africa's New Big Man Rule," 15.

23. McCauley, "Africa's New Big Man Rule," 14.

24. Recent surveys of the political influence of Pentecostalism in the Global South include Lende, "Rise of Pentecostal Power," and Lindhardt, *Pentecostalism in Africa*.

25. Robbins, "Globalization," 127.

26. Robbins, "Globalization," 129.

27. Casanova, "Religion, the New Millennium," 438.

28. Robbins, "Globalization," 130–31.

tion or formal credentials. In a similar vein, Anderson highlights contextual leadership as one of the central features of Pentecostal mission, noting that Pentecostalism is flexible in adopting and developing local forms of leadership and leadership development on the mission field.[29] By downplaying formal requirements, the movement is able to draw from a large pool of local talent where most converts may serve in some capacity. This emphasis on national people sent by the Spirit, claims Anderson, is a fundamental difference between Pentecostal and traditional missions.

In summing up this section, I concur with Samuel's assertion that the promotion of indigenous leadership is a common characteristic of the diverse and complex global Pentecostal movement.[30] The accentuation on local and contextual leadership is one of the reasons for the movement's remarkable growth and expansion across very different settings. In Latin-America, cultural dimensions have merged with Pentecostal theology and created what Matviuk perceives to be a Latin American Pentecostal leadership and church growth strategy, resulting in an apprentice system that reflects local cultural values.[31] From an African perspective, Easter advocates approaches that balance contextual awareness and adaptation of local practices with principles of biblical leadership, including experiential, incarnational, and participatory modes of learning geared toward missional transformation.[32] These are mere examples. The contextual nature of Pentecostal leadership comes with the danger of being blindsided by destructive elements in the host culture, yet there are obvious benefits. For instance, research indicates that indigenous leadership makes Pentecostal churches in the majority world better suited to bring deep-rooted and long-lasting change in society than international nongovernmental organizations, because they are more embedded in the local context than their secular counterparts.[33] Further, the spiritual dynamics of Pentecostalism have minimized the distinction between clergy and laity and rediscovered the giftedness and contribution of each individual member through the power of the Spirit. This has bolstered the development of national leadership in Pentecostal mission, and represents a key contribution for the growth of global Pentecostalism.[34]

29. Anderson, "Patterns," 17–20.
30. Samuel, "Pentecostalism as a Global Culture," 253.
31. Matviuk, "Pentecostal Leadership Development."
32. Easter, "Under the Mango Tree."
33. Myers, "Progressive Pentecostalism," 118.
34. Klaus and Triplett, "National Leadership," 225–26, 233–35.

Charismatic and Enigmatically Powerful

Several constructs of organizational leadership have been utilized to describe leadership in Pentecostalism. For example, Austin argued that leaders in the Mongolian Pentecostal movement display transformational leadership behaviors, and that this leadership may have assisted in the rapid growth of Pentecostalism in the country.[35] Further, Fogarty empirically investigated the impact of transactional and transformational leadership behaviors of Australian Pentecostal pastors on volunteer motivation, and found that senior pastors who engage in transformational leadership behaviors are likely to have longer tenure and lead larger congregations, and inspire greater trust, value congruence, and intrinsic motivation among volunteers.[36] In another paper, Fogarty described the Korean Pentecostal leader David Yonggi Cho by means of servant-leadership theory, insisting that Cho's leader effectiveness is related to his ability to integrate servant leadership with the example of Jesus and a Christian understanding of the relational nature of the triune God.[37]

However, it is Max Weber's concept of charisma that is most frequently used to describe leadership within the Pentecostal movement; Klaus even suggests charismatic leadership as a Pentecostal default position.[38] Charisma, one of Weber's three pure types of authority, is dynamic and personal compared to the two other and more stable authority bases (traditional and legal-rational). Weber describes charisma as "a certain quality of an individual personality by virtue of which he is set apart from ordinary men and treated as endowed with supernatural, superhuman, or at least specifically exceptional qualities."[39] Charisma may have both psychological and sociological elements, and Weber incorporated both in his definition.[40] The psychological perspective is individualistically oriented and suggests that charisma evolves from inner dynamics in the leader's personality. The sociological perspective, in contrast, highlights how charismatic authority depends on the recognition of a group of people. The two perspectives are not mutually exclusive because "leaders depend upon the perceptions of people

35. Austin, "Decreed by Heaven."

36. Fogarty, "Transformational and Transactional Leadership."

37. Fogarty, "Servant Leadership."

38. Klaus, "Implications of Globalization," 144.

39. Weber, *On Charisma and Institution Building*, 48.

40. Barnes, "Charisma and Religious Leadership," 1.

for their charismatic authority, but nonetheless they also must be exceptional to gain such recognition."[41] Either way, charisma typically emerges in times of crisis or social turmoil. If the leader is no longer perceived as charismatic, the source of authority will quickly erode, with the potential of organizational collapse, as witnessed by Poloma and Hood in their sad description of David VanCronkhite's leadership of a neo-Pentecostal ministry in Atlanta, Georgia.[42]

Heuser and Klaus suggest that charismatic leadership is prone to emerge in contexts where supernaturalistic sentiments are present—such as in Pentecostalism—and the construct is a widespread companion to study leadership in the movement.[43] For instance, Repstad relies on the notion of charisma in describing leadership in the Norwegian Pentecostal movement, and shows how leadership in this context is typically happening in a tension between the leader's personal charisma and more institutionalized authority based on both democracy and expertise.[44] The literature also describes the leadership of the two giants in Scandinavian Pentecostalism, Thomas Ball Barratt and Lewi Pethrus, as charismatic leaders.[45] In line with Smith's claim that the communication of a narrative addressing ultimate concern is crucial for the rise of charisma,[46] Åkerlund contends that Barratt's telling of his Spirit baptism was essential to his leadership in the European Pentecostal movement. In Barratt's experience—and the narration of it—theological and sociological themes merged in a way that made sense to many people. The importance of the event and the following revival bolstered Barratt's leadership; as his message carried ultimate and eschatological weight, so did the messenger. This connection between encounters with the Spirit and leadership carries particular weight in Pentecostal churches, since it is more common to claim direct inspiration from God—including divine authorization of one's message and leadership—in Pentecostalism than in other Christian traditions.[47]

The Pentecostal predisposal to strong leaders with charismatic tendencies does not automatically lead to the marginalization of the average

41. Barnes, "Charisma and Religious Leadership."
42. See Poloma and Hood, *Blood and Fire*.
43. Heuser and Klaus, "Charismatic Leadership Theory."
44. Repstad, "Mellom Karisma og Kontor."
45. Åkerlund, "When the Fire Fell"; Lindberg, "Swedish Pentecostal Movement."
46. Smith, "Culture and Charisma," 102–3.
47. Leoh, "Pentecostal Preacher," 53–56.

believer, however. Numerous works have been written about the empower-ment of traditionally and culturally marginalized groups within Pentecos-talism, such as women[48] and the handicapped.[49] This is not the place to go into detail on any of these issues, but it is necessary to highlight how the elevation of the marginalized has been a central part of the Pentecostal story since its inception. The result is a leveling of the field, so to speak, epitomized by developments in the Global South where the Pentecostal movement has "succeeded in turning the losers of society into winners, a chosen people that enjoys spiritual privileges and exercises spiritual authority."[50] It is this paradox consisting of a few individuals in charge com-bined with the enabling of the many, of strong leaders in co-existence with empowerment of marginalized groups, that I have in mind when I describe Pentecostal leadership as enigmatic and powerful in this section. In the past, some observers have emphasized the democratic potential inherent in the movement, while others have argued that it represents nothing but a symbolic subversion of traditional social order.[51] I believe that this is a false dichotomy, because the tension between egalitarian and authoritarian impulses is latent in Pentecostal leadership, and both aspects should be ac-counted for to avoid one-sided descriptions of the phenomenon.

As an illustration, Miller and Yamamori noticed the tension between Pentecostal leaders with strong personal charisma on one side and the em-powerment of the people on the other in their study of neo-Pentecostal groups.[52] The senior pastors in first-generation churches were typically charismatic, dynamic, and even authoritarian. Yet, the churches embraced priesthood of all believers and the idea that ministry work is done by the laity. Again, this question of how strong hierarchical leadership can fit with active lay leadership represents an enigma for Pentecostal leadership.

On one hand, charismatic leaders pose a challenge because people are attracted to the person rather than to the church and its vision. This personal magnetism carries the seed of potential pathologies of autocratic leadership on the individual as well as the congregational level, described by Heuser and Klaus as the shadow side of charismatic leadership.[53] Through a

---

48. Alexander and Yong, *Philip's Daughters*; Gunnestad, "Kvinner i Lederskap"; Pow-ers, "Your Daughters Shall Prophesy."

49. Fettke, "Spirit of God"; Yong, "Disability."

50. Lindhardt, *Power in Powerlessness*, 6.

51. See brief discussion in Robbins, "Globalization," 134–35.

52. Miller and Yamamori, *Global Pentecostalism*.

53. Heuser and Klaus, "Charismatic Leadership Theory."

series of interviews, Miller and Yamamori found that the leaders of highly successful congregations were confident and creative, giving little room to consensual process, or drifted away from the vision they had received from God. The authors hence warn that "the long-term challenge for leaders with intense personal charisma is to continue as a visionary leader while simultaneously giving the ministry to the people to embrace as their own."[54] On the other hand, Progressive Pentecostals represent a renewal movement that breaks with hierarchical organizational structures, democratizes involvement and lay participation, and encourages direct experience of the holy. Miller and Yamamori reported that many of the senior pastors were very approachable and themselves products of the social contexts in which the congregations were located and therefore able to respond to the needs of the churches as well as the wider communities. Many of the churches also had flat organizational structures with homegrown leaders and an emphasis on enabling others to do the work of ministry. Despite the emphasis on strong charismatic leaders within the Pentecostal ranks, then, Miller and Yamamori describe the organization of many growing Pentecostal churches in terms of organic rather than hierarchical imagery, the body metaphor being the prime example. The discovery and use of the spiritual gifts were the driving organizational principle in the churches they studied. It follows that the tasks of leaders are to enable, mentor, and nurture people as they exercised their gifts for the common good.

These characteristics lead Miller and Yamamori to compare the organizing of these churches with innovative, cutting-edge technology companies where collaboration is preferred over hierarchy.[55] While senior leadership typically inhabits the role of trendsetters, there are high degrees of flexibility and trust and little emphasis on degrees, titles, and appearance. Notably, Miller and Yamamori found that neo-Pentecostal churches were organizationally more progressive than their classical siblings, probably due to the routinizations of leadership in the older congregations. While the same is prone to happen in many newer churches over time, the present state of Progressive Pentecostalism provides fresh perspectives on how charisma and lay involvement may exist in creative tension in Pentecostal settings.

Campos addresses the dilemma of strong leaders versus empowered people from a slightly different perspective.[56] On one side, the author re-

---

54. Miller and Yamamori, *Global Pentecostalism*, 188.

55. Miller and Yamamori, *Global Pentecostalism*, 190.

56. Campos, "Sharing Charisma."

marks that Brazilian Pentecostal leaders are celebrities of faith, even to the point that their preaching functions as a mediation between believers and the divine, marking a shift in authority from Scripture to the ecclesial leader. On the other side, this seeming reinvention of hierarchy based on the extraordinary abilities of the leader also represents a sharing of charisma, as it extends beyond the individual(s) in charge. To understand the authority of Pentecostal charisma, then, one must understand how charisma is learned, transmitted, and shared because these aspects are fundamental to the global spread of Pentecostalism. According to Campos, charisma flows in three directions: (a) through commodification (i.e., the charisma of the leader becomes material commodity in the form of paid conferences, courses, CDs/DVDs, etc.), (b) family names (i.e., transmission of charisma along kinship lines), and (c) emotional and bodily channeling of energy between leaders and believers. By mimicking the leader, believers get access to his or her charisma:

> The faithful want charisma for themselves; they want to be empowered. Being empowered may be related to a desire for domination, to become a leader. However, it also may be related to another kind of desire: to live well and to acquire the signs of salvation. It is this circulation between the pastor and believers that is the main form of transmission of charisma. The confirmation of charismatic authority relies on such a circulation.[57]

It follows that the leader's ability to disseminate charisma is crucial to Pentecostalism and its global expansion. The movement's main institutional base is the word of God, and those who spread the message do not have to belong to any ecclesial hierarchy. Lacking any single or centralized foundation, every believer can evangelize and thereby mimic the leader among friends and neighbors. Despite the emergence of charismatic leaders, then, there is seemingly open access to charisma in Pentecostalism.

The distribution of the *charismata*, or the spiritual gifts, underscores the notion that every believer is called and empowered for ministry. It is through this open access to the gifts of the Spirit that individual believers can lay claim on different ministries, including those involving leadership, such as evangelists, teachers, prophets, apostles, and pastors.[58] In Pentecostalism, empowerment—to be "resourced or made capable of achieving aims and accomplishing feats that would otherwise have remained difficult

57. Campos, "Sharing Charisma," 284.
58. Asamoah-Gyadu, "You Shall Receive Power," 64.

or impossible to undertake"[59]—is synonymous with the presence of the Spirit as the power and authority of God.[60] Asamoah-Gyadu notes how this understanding of the believer's direct access to God is formative for Pentecostalism's distinct ecclesiology, as it undermines any need for priestly meditation. By implication, at least in theory, every individual has the same opportunity to receive and experience the charismatic gifts. This notion of divine intervention represents a radical reworking of the universal priesthood, and is a key to the expansion of Pentecostalism around the world.[61] By emphasizing baptism in the Holy Spirit, Pentecostalism has added a dimension to the Lutheran doctrine of the priesthood of all believers:[62] The Spirit empowers believers to effective ministry and enables them to serve beyond their natural abilities. Such emphasis on spiritual empowerment over formal education downplays traditional credentials, elevates practical and experiential learning, and provides the Pentecostal congregations with a large—and local—pool of talent they can draw from.

However, while Pentecostalism is democratic in the sense that charisma is open to everyone, stratification occurs because some figures are seen as more exemplary than others. In this aspect, charismatic leaders in Pentecostalism have roles parallel to saints in the Catholic tradition.[63] The exemplary power of charismatic leaders is bolstered by what Campos perceives to be a lack of interest in the Bible in Pentecostal circles. When the charismatic leader transforms the biblical text into something alive and tangible, he or she replaces the authority of Scripture itself. Charisma is thus understood and shared as mimesis of the leader, meaning that success for the charismatic leader is ensured through the capacity for performative transmission of his or her charisma through bodily synchrony with believers. In conclusion, Campos contends that Pentecostal leaders

---

59. Asamoah-Gyadu, "You Shall Receive Power," 46–47.

60. Järvinen ("Equipping and Empowering") notes that empowerment is a slippery term with no consensus definition. The unique Pentecostal understanding supersedes psychological and sociological explanation by insisting that the source of power is beyond any human agent or institution. Part of the paradox depicted in the review between charismatic leadership and lay empowerment, arguably stems from the fact that both phenomena points to spiritual empowerment for justification.

61. Järvinen, "Equipping and Empowering," 179; Kärkkäinen, "Taking Stock," xiv–xv; Sun, "Missing Key," 183–89.

62. Sun, "Missing Key."

63. See Coleman, "Transgressing the Self."

are teaching not only a new language to their congregations and their audiences, but also a new way of interpreting reality, of living according to the Word in relation to other people and objects and thus of (re)imagining their communities. They are granted divine authority by virtue of their ability to make charisma circulate, creating forms of alliances and communities that strengthen the process of "reaching out."[64]

The unstable nature of charismatic leadership, as discussed, moderates the autocratic tendencies in Pentecostal leadership. If the charismatic individual is no longer perceived as an extraordinary individual endowed with special capacities, the source of authority will quickly erode. This ambiguous nature of charisma is evident in Währisch-Oblau's study of leaders in Pentecostal migrant churches. While the claim to leadership in these settings is authority-sounding in theory, it is relatively democratic in practice because members submit to the pastor by free will and consequently are free to leave if they no longer respect the leader's authority. "The pastor who claims to have received a call cannot rest on it. He needs to be persistent in maintaining a spiritual life that gives him a clear understanding of the divine will in concrete situations."[65] Hence, charisma is not an attribute of the leader alone but is intertwined with situational and contextual factors as well as perceptual and attributional processes among followers.[66]

What is important to recognize, then, is the latent tension between a radical open egalitarianism (all have the same access to the empowering Spirit) and the notions of hierarchy and submission (the Spirit has empowered some to lead). Währisch-Oblau suggests that this stems from an underdeveloped ecclesiology:

> On the one hand, pastors see themselves as imbued with special authority by the Holy Spirit—a clearly hierarchical idea. On the other hand, the understanding of the spiritual gifts is "anarchic" in the sense that the gifts are not tied to a certain office.[67]

Although present, the tension between the authority of leaders and the empowerment and participation of all seems to be eased by the communal focus of Pentecostalism: "In this ecclesiological mindset, the Spirit poured

64. Campos, "Sharing Charisma," 287.

65. Währisch-Oblau, *Missionary Self-Perception*, 130.

66. Beyer, "Taming and Promoting Charisma"; Joosse, "Max Weber"; see also Joosse, "Becoming a God."

67. Währisch-Oblau, *Missionary Self-Perception*, 82.

out on all flesh leads not only to the charismatic endowment of all believers but ultimately to a charismatic church."[68] The gifted congregation, not merely the anointed individual, is a hallmark of Pentecostal theology.[69]

This is not to say that egalitarianism is realized. Tensions between notions of equality drawn from the life in the Spirit and cultural conventions drawn from the wider context in which the community exists complicate the picture. Regarding gender issues, for instance, Vondey contends that the movement simultaneously is characterized by revolutionary egalitarianism and fundamentalist, conservative chauvinist attitudes.[70] This gender paradox is especially visible in patriarchal societies.[71] Despite these challenges, Vondey insists that Pentecostalism is essentially a movement toward an egalitarian and democratic identity, but that this development is hampered by the high degrees of institutionalism that go with emergence of the movement. The conflict between spiritual egalitarianism and ecclesial pragmatism, individual empowerment and institutional practices, continues to haunt the Pentecostal movement and hinder the potential egalitarianism of its ethos to be realized in its polity. It is hence best described as "an egalitarian movement in-the-making."[72]

Summary

It is clear that studies on Pentecostal leadership are in their infancy. As research on spiritual leadership and spirituality in organizational leadership gains momentum, the intensifying of inquiry into leadership of the movement that has evoked the largest shift on the global religious scene over the last century is overdue.

---

68. Vondey, *Pentecostalism*, 117.

69. Macchia, "Theology, Pentecostal," 1137.

70. Vondey, *Pentecostalism*, 111–31.

71. Robbins notes how Pentecostalism recognizes two sources of authority, institutional and inspirational ("Globalization," 132). Men typically inhabit institutional roles, such as pastors, while women work as lay preachers, evangelists, and other public settings based on spiritual gifts and inspirational authority. These settings open the door for women to develop public leadership skills—even in patriarchal societies, where such involvement is socially and culturally discouraged. This may partly explain the numerous examples of entrepreneurial leaders, but only one female pastor, in Miller and Yamamori's study on Progressive Pentecostalism.

72. Vondey, *Pentecostalism*, 131.

Two points may serve as a springboard from the extant body of research to the following phenomenological study. First, Pentecostal leadership—as Pentecostalism, in general—is highly contextual and pragmatic, drawing from local cultures as well as its distinct spiritual repertoire. The differing models of leadership and organizing reflect the movement's ability to adapt to local demands and environments and their uses of market strategies and entrepreneurial tools.[73]

This diversity represents both an incitement to study Pentecostal leadership in local contexts and a caution to make monolithic claims about the nature of the phenomenon. Negatively, one cannot take for granted that characteristics of Pentecostal leadership in Norway will be the same in other places. Positively, this inherent ambiguity makes it crucial to provide descriptions from local leaders to reveal potentially unaddressed aspects of the phenomenon.

Second, there is a general lack of empirical research into how leaders in the Pentecostal movement understand their leadership. Cartledge laments this relative absence of rigorous empirical research on Pentecostalism from a practical theology perspective and fears that it results in failure "to explore and map the actual theological praxis of Pentecostals themselves, that is, the theology embedded in their beliefs, values, and practices."[74] As a result, researchers have offered merely an applicationist model of practical theology that replicates standard evangelical seminary education rather than distinct Pentecostal approach to theology and praxis. The same is true from an organizational leadership perspective, where extant research primarily draws on established, a priori analytical frameworks rather than letting patterns emerge from the data itself. The various descriptions of the Korean Pentecostal pastor David Yonggi Cho illustrate the inadequacy of relying on mainstream leadership constructs in studies of Pentecostal leadership. Fogarty shows that the literature describes Cho as a charismatic, transcendent, or spiritual leader.[75] Fogarty, on the other hand, argues for Cho's servant leadership. May the real leadership theory please stand up!

To be fair, leadership is a multidimensional construct, and the various theories arguably shed light on the same phenomenon from different vantage points. Yet, the risk of reading a theoretical framework back into the data is immanent when the researcher uses analytical constructs

73. Anderson et al., *Studying Global Pentecostalism*, 2.
74. Cartledge, "Practical Theology," 282.
75. Fogarty, "Servant Leadership."

developed elsewhere for studies on Pentecostalism. In Hacking's words, "our preserved theories and the world fit together so snugly less because we have found out how the world is than because we have tailored each to the other."[76] Smith warns particularly about the insufficiency of current categories and paradigms in explaining Pentecostalism.[77] Tangen's discussion on the usefulness of charisma is interesting in this regard.[78] While affirming the value of Weber's framework, Tangen warns against reductionistic portrayals of Pentecostal leadership when relying solely on sociological constructs that do not sufficiently take into consideration the theological aspects of charisma. This is not the place to discuss various understandings of charisma and their relevance for study on Pentecostalism. The point is rather that existing constructs should be handled with care so that new insights are allowed to emerge from data derived from empirical studies on Pentecostal leadership.

What is largely lacking in the current discourse is an emic description of the phenomenon through the eyes of Pentecostal leaders themselves. This speaks in favor of the phenomenological approach, which aims at describing the essential meaning of a phenomenon in terms of subjective lived experience. As described in the introductory chapter, the current study seeks to answer the questions of meaning of Pentecostal leadership for pastors in the Norwegian Pentecostal movement. For meaning to appear, however, means of its appearance must be addressed. The quest for scientific understanding leads to the question of scientific method—and to this the study now turns.

76. Quoted in Deininger, *Global Pentecostalism*, 5.
77. Smith, *Thinking in Tongues*.
78. Tangen, "Karismatisk Ledelse."

PART 2

A Phenomenology Of Pentecostal Leadership

4

An Introduction to Method

HAVING REVIEWED AND SYSTEMATIZED the present understanding of Pentecostal leadership in the first part of the book, this second part expands our knowledge of the subject by reporting the results of a phenomenological study seeking to explicate the lived meaning of leadership among pastors in the movement. Prior to looking at—and discussing—these findings, it is necessary to briefly spell out the philosophical assumptions, methodological concerns, and practical steps that guided data collection and analysis. In the following, philosophical assumptions are briefly discussed before Husserl's phenomenology is addressed. Finally, Giorgi's modified Husserlian method and its consequences are introduced and spelled out in practical steps. This way, the rationale behind the research process and the steps leading to its findings are made stringent and transparent, increasing the rigor of the study.

Philosophical Assumptions

Phenomenology, a movement first in European continental philosophy and later in behavioral research, was founded by the German philosopher Edmund Husserl.[1] With Kant and Hegel—and especially Bretano—as

1. While Husserl undoubtedly was the founder of the phenomenology, his followers questioned some of his views (e.g., the possibility and necessity of bracketing), and developed the program along other paths than those embraced by its founding father. Consequently, the broader phenomenological movement came to extend beyond the works of Husserl. Moran argues that phenomenology came to be seen as the combined contribution

important forerunners, it was Husserl who formally introduced this new way of doing philosophy at the outset of the twentieth century. From its beginning, the program of phenomenology sought to revitalize philosophy by returning it to the lived experience of the human subject.[2] From a phenomenological vantage point, it is through the studies of lived experience that one comes to understand phenomena—and thereby aspects of reality. What phenomenology proposes is an alternative theory of experience where the interest is on reality's impact on human beings rather than brute facts—"a shift of focus away from the thing and nature toward human beings and their world."[3] People embody the world, and their experience of reality is important as it reveals the social reality the researcher aims to describe. As such, phenomenology is a "philosophy of attention."[4]

In terms of positioning within the landscape of empirical research strategies, phenomenology finds a middle ground between two extremes:

> On the one hand, the neo-positivist objectivism that a-critically assumes the existence of objects in the world and believes in the possibility of discovering universal laws that govern them; and on the other hand, a postmodern subjectivism, skeptical and relativistic, that denies the possibility of rigorous thinking about the world, and thwarts the urges to investigate the phenomena beyond their discursive construction.[5]

Giorgi argues in a similar way when he describes phenomenology as distinct from positivist and naturalist (constructivist) paradigms.[6] Whereas the positivist holds a view of reality as single, tangible, and fragmented, and the naturalist advocates multiple and constructed realities, Giorgi suggests that reality statements are not made but instead present themselves through description. The relationship between the knower and the known is thus not independent (as in positivism) or inseparable (as in naturalism), but related to the principle of intentionality. In distancing phenomenology from both positivist objectivism and postmodern relativism, Giorgi

---

of both Husserl and Heidegger after the latter's publication of *Being and Time* in 1927, and that this understanding was dominant for the later phenomenologists Levinas, Sartre, Merleau-Ponty, and Derrida. See Moran, *Introduction to Phenomenology*, 2.

2. Moran, *Introduction to Phenomenology*, 4.

3. Giorgi, "Phenomenological Movement," 76.

4. Mortari and Tarozzi, "Phenomenology as Philosophy," 19.

5. Mortari and Tarozzi, "Phenomenology as Philosophy," 22.

6. Giorgi, "Phenomenological Perspective," 201–6.

allows for a reality independent of the researcher while admitting that one's knowledge of the world is subjectively and socially constituted.

> The phenomenological approach admits to a reality independent of consciousness but claims that knowledge of such reality can only come through consciousness of it, so it is better to study the reality claims made by persons through their consciousness of it.[7]

In other words, phenomenology does not present a mirror of reality, as in naïve realism, but rather explores how human beings experience things. It represents a return to the phenomena precisely because it is in appearance that being discloses itself. The sphere of experience is structured and appears at the intersection between world and person, and it is the aim of phenomenological research to examine the processes that give a phenomenon meaning and structure in consciousness.[8] Consequently, it is the researcher's task to be concerned with what appears through a careful description of the phenomenon, rather than speculating about casual explanations. Since relevant data are to be found in the perspectives of individuals who experience a phenomenon (e.g., Pentecostal leadership), the researcher needs to engage with participants in collecting data.

Descriptive Phenomenological Methodology

Since phenomenology is a diverse phenomenon, it is necessary to be explicit about what stance is followed when doing phenomenological research. Central phenomenologists such as Husserl, Heidegger, and Merleau-Ponty never elaborated the consequences of their ontology and ideas for empirical research, but instead remained strictly philosophical. This does not mean that the researcher may freely pick and choose from the smorgasbord in the phenomenological cafeteria. On the contrary, each approach comes with a specific set of assumptions, and a commitment and sensibility to the integrity of each strategy is needed. The reliance upon and strong link to philosophy mean that a researcher using the phenomenological method needs to have at least a minimum understanding of phenomenological philosophy. Consequently, the ideas of Husserl must be addressed before descriptive phenomenology, as described by Giorgi, will be applied as a research method in this study.

7. Giorgi, "Phenomenological Perspective," 2003.
8. Polkinghorne, "Phenomenological Research Methods," 51.

Husserl's Phenomenology

Husserl's project was to restore philosophy as a central discipline by re-turning to its original ideal of pursuit of absolute knowledge in terms of comprehending the essential nature of reality. Holding that all knowledge was derived from experience, and that access to the world was through consciousness, Husserl proposed phenomenology as a method to reach certainty through descriptions of essences of a phenomenon.[9] For Hus-serl, phenomenological analysis can only start by turning attention to the phenomenon—epitomized in his famous dictum "we must go back to the 'things themselves.'"[10] This stance draws attention to the need for descrip-tions of what is immediately given in experience without any interference from preconceptions or theoretical notions. Phenomenology, then, is the study of structures of a phenomenon as it appears to consciousness.[11] As-pects of Husserl's phenomenological method, important for this study, are briefly outlined below.

Intentionality

The concept of intentionality is a key to Husserl's thinking.[12] First intro-duced by Bretano and later developed by Husserl, intentionality means "to be conscious of something";[13] that is, the way one reaches out to events in the world and make sense of them. Consciousness enjoys a privileged status within phenomenology because it cannot be avoided, and is consequently understood as the medium of access to everything given to awareness.[14] Yet, we are never simply conscious. Human consciousness is directional, point-ing to some object—it is "'consciousness-of' something; it always 'intends' something, or is 'about' something."[15] The act and object of consciousness are intentionally connected; while the act of consciousness is directed to an object, and the object transcends that act.[16]

9. Priest, "Phenomenological Analysis," 51. See also Husserl, *Ideas*.

10. Husserl, *Shorter Logical Investigations*, 88.

11. Giorgi, *Descriptive Phenomenological Method*.

12. Zahavi, *Husserl's Phenomenology*, 3, 13–22.

13. Husserl, *Ideas*, 171.

14. Giorgi, "Theory, Practice, and Evaluation," 236.

15. Jennings, "Husserl Revisited," 1236.

16. Giorgi, "Theory, Practice, and Evaluation," 238.

By demonstrating the unity between things and consciousness, Husserl sought to heal the Cartesian subject-object split: "We are not doomed like Decartes to think only our own thoughts,"[17] but are intuitively connected to the object—although from a perspective and not with a God's-eye view. The object of interest can be real, imaginary, or conceptual, but the starting point is always conscious awareness with the intentional directing of focus to describe particular realities. This way, the researcher may get insight into the structures of a person's consciousness—structures described by Husserl as essences, another important aspect of his philosophy, in order to arrive at "comprehensive descriptions of the essential nature of things."[18] However, some steps must be followed.

Phenomenological reduction

Husserl's method incorporates several reductions and different levels of reduction;[19] two of which are particularly important for the present work. The first is phenomenological reduction, which means that pre-reflective attitudes and preconceptions must be exposed and held in abeyance to retrieve an original and nonjudgmental stance toward a phenomenon. "The *reduction*, or *epoché*, is a radical self-meditative process whereby the philosopher brackets (puts aside) the natural, taken-for-granted everyday world and any interpretations in order to let the phenomenon show itself in its essence."[20] A radical shift in viewpoint is necessary to insure that explanations are not imposed before a phenomenon is understood from within.[21] To achieve this, Husserl proposed a radical alternation of the "natural standpoint" or the "attitude"[22]—that is, "our tendency to immediately accept the surrounding environment as something that really exists out there and that provides a fixed reality shared by others."[23] This natural attitude should not be uncritically accepted, but rather tested thoroughly to ensure

17. Røseth et al., "Engulfed," 156. See also Sokolowski, *Introduction to Phenomenology*, 8–16.

18. Husserl, *Ideas*, 144.

19. Føllesdal, "Husserl's Reductions."

20. Finlay, "Engaging Phenomenological Analysis," 122.

21. Moran, *Introduction to Phenomenology*, 1–4.

22. Husserl, *Ideas*, 51–60.

23. Jennings, "Husserl Revisited," 1237. See also Sokolowski, *Introduction to Phenomenology*, 42–47.

that our investigation is guided by what is given, rather than by our *a priori* commitments. Consequently, "phenomenology demands of us re-learning to look at the world as we meet it in immediate experience."[24]

Through reduction, the researcher transcends the natural attitude and reaches the phenomenological attitude. This is necessary to achieve a receptive attitude toward the phenomenon and to create a void in the mind to receive the datum without pressing it into preconceived grids and concepts, and enables the phenomenologists to understand the natural attitude and the lifeworld of the participant better than it understands itself.[25] To do so, the researcher keeps the natural attitude with the purpose of investigating it, but brackets its validity to avoid its natural inclination—"we keep them as they are, but we contemplate them."[26] As a metaphor taken from mathematics, bracketing involves setting one's natural understanding of the world in brackets in order to place it temporarily out of question.[27] The goal is not to neglect or deny reality, but to neutralize a certain attitude toward it, through what Husserl described as *epoché*.

This attitudinal shift enables the researcher to study the phenomenon from a fresh perspective without imposing meaning to it, and directs attention to how it is experienced by the participant. The focus shifts from the object that appears to its manner of appearing.[28] By attending to how the phenomenon presents itself to consciousness, the researcher can grasp the structure of the phenomenon. It follows that open attention is required of the phenomenological researcher, and *epoché* works toward silencing available references, scientific as well as ordinary. This way, the phenomenologist remains open to how the phenomenon manifests itself instead of being pre-oriented to look for something particular. Through bracketing, Husserl believed that it was possible to comprehend

24. Van Manen, *Researching Lived Experience*, 184.

25. Giorgi, "Status of Husserlian Phenomenology," 6.

26. Sokolowski, *Introduction to Phenomenology*, 48.

27. Whether bracketing is useful (or possible) marks a schism between descriptive and hermeneutic phenomenology. Heidegger rejects the idea of phenomenological reduction and argues for an interpretive process in which it is neither possible nor desirable to bracket out preconceptions; see Gearing, "Bracketing in Research," 1431, and Walters, "Phenomenological Movement." Instead, Heidegger emphasizes engagement as a means of knowing, an idea carried out in participatory action research; Tufford and Newman, "Bracketing in Qualitative Research," 82–83.

28. Reeder, *Theory and Practice*, 26.

the common features and true nature of any phenomenon—referred to as universal essences or eidetic structures[29]—to be discussed next.

Eidetic reduction

Phenomenologists do not merely attempt to provide descriptions of experience, but aim for accounts of the essential features of a phenomenon. Put differently, the goal is not merely to study people's subjective experiences but to go beneath and beyond how they usually describe what they experience to the structures that underlie them. As such, the focus of phenomenological investigation lies with the phenomenon itself, and not primarily with the individual experiences of it.

In this regard, Husserl proposes a second reduction—the eidetic reduction—to concentrate on the essential nature of objects. "The *eidetic reduction* is the transition from the *natural* attitude, where we are directed toward particular material objects, to the *eidetic* attitude, where we are directed toward essences."[30] For Husserl, essence (or *eidos*) is not something unique for each object, but something that is shared among many objects. Thus, the eidetic reduction is "a process whereby a particular object is reduced to its essence,"[31] a turning away from studying specific objects to general features.

The outcome of a phenomenological analysis is ultimately to determine the meaning of experience.[32] In Husserlian phenomenology, this comes in the form of a description of the essential structure of the phenomenon being studied, "the elements or constituents that are necessary for an experience to present itself as what it is."[33] This happens through free imaginative variation, a process where the researcher changes aspects or parts of a phenomenon to see whether it remains identifiable with the part changed or not.[34] In time, the variation will lead the researcher to certain characteristics that cannot be varied without the object ceasing to be what it is. According to Husserl, then,

29. Wojnar and Swanson, "Phenomenology: An Exploration," 174.

30. Føllesdal, "Husserl's Reductions," 110.

31. Giorgi, *Descriptive Phenomenological Method*, 90.

32. Giorgi and Giorgi, "Descriptive Phenomenological Psychological Method," 252.

33. Polkinghorne, "Phenomenological Research Methods," 51.

34. Zaner, "At Play"; Giorgi, "Theory, Practice, and Evaluation," 242.

I can obtain an essential insight, a *Wesensschau*, if through an eidetic variation, I succeed in establishing the horizon within which the object can change without losing its identity as a thing of that type. In that case, I will have succeeded in disclosing the invariant structure that make up its essence.[35]

Giorgi's descriptive phenomenological method, to be discussed next, seeks to explicate the meanings already there in the participant's experience of the world—to bring to light that which is present but hidden in the natural attitude toward the world and the phenomenon. Describing essences is, therefore, the clarification of meaning as it is given.

The Descriptive Phenomenological Method

Giorgi belongs to the Duquesne School of phenomenology, which has developed a branch of psychology that draws on phenomenological philosophy. This phenomenological method is an attempt to translate Husserl's—and partly Merleau-Ponty's—philosophical phenomenology into a program of scientific (psychological) research. The approach is descriptive in two ways—first, because it takes the participant's everyday descriptions of an experience, and then because it ends in a second-order description of essence or structure by the researcher. Giorgi's goal is to generate accurate descriptions of the structure of the human experience, mainly based on descriptions provided by individuals other than the researcher. This is achieved through the phenomenological method that, generically, consists of three interlocking aspects or processes, all necessary for a method to be considered phenomenological in the Husserlian sense:[36]

First, the researcher must describe the phenomenon that is studied precisely as it presents itself, without adding or subtracting anything from it. Second, such a description can only take place in an attitude of phenomenological reduction. This means that the researcher holds back existential approval of the phenomenon and brackets of all theories or prior knowledge about it. Finally, the researcher begins the search for essences after the initial steps of description within an attitude of reduction are performed. The goal is for invariant and essential characteristics to show themselves so that the researcher can describe them and their

35. Zahavi, *Husserl's Phenomenology*, 39.
36. Giorgi, "Theory, Practice, and Evaluation."

relationship to each other. This description, then, becomes the essential structure of the phenomenon.

Data Collection

Phenomenological researchers prefer interviewing as the dominant method of data collection, because they are interested in the meaning of a phenomenon as it is lived and experienced through human beings. Since rich and nuanced descriptions, rather than categorization, was the focus of the interview, I invited the interviewee to focus on specific situations he had experienced to avoid data that were too abstract and general or expressed options and attitudes rather than experiences. The goal was for the participant to describe his lived experience, not to interpret it.[37]

"Leadership" is an ambiguous term, and the introductory interview question used the verb "to lead" in order to draw attention to the participants' experience of leadership in Pentecostalism. An opening question was hence posed as follows: "Can you describe as detailed as possible a situation in which you experienced 'to lead' in a Pentecostal church?" To avoid dithering conversations, the interview was terminated when the participant had reached a level of saturation in talking about his experiences of Pentecostal leadership, meaning the interview had come to the point where further descriptions were not possible in the given situation.[38]

In-depth interviews were conducted in January–March 2016, all face to face in the participants' native language (Norwegian) to ensure rich descriptions and eliminate misunderstandings due to language barriers. Only full-text quotes reported in the study were later translated into English. Since the aim was eidetic and not empirical generalizations, four male pastors[39] in three fairly large churches in southern Norway were con-

---

37. Roulston, *Reflective Interviewing*, 17.

38. Englander, "Interview," 31. "Saturation" here relates to the interview situation, not to sampling procedures. The concept of data saturation was originally developed for grounded method, and rests on empirical rather than phenomenological assumptions. Though sometimes used in phenomenological studies, Giorgi (personal communication, November 25, 2015) holds that the notion of data saturation is less meaningful in studies following a Husserlian approach. This is because the descriptive phenomenological method includes imaginative variation where the researcher always goes beyond the empirical givens.

39. Given the fact that there are very few female pastors in the Norwegian Pentecostal movement, no women were included, since participation would jeopardize their

sidered a sufficient number of participants because they all provided rich descriptions of Pentecostal leadership.[40] By recruiting leaders with at least five years of pastoral experience in Pentecostal congregations, Pentecostal leadership was framed organizationally as the ministry of pastors in the Norwegian Pentecostal movement. This is a heuristic move, and does not indicate that leadership is limited to formal positions.

Data Analysis

Interview data were analyzed following Giorgi's descriptive phenomenological method in psychology, a modified Husserlian approach that attempts to translate philosophical phenomenology to serve social and human scientific purposes.[41] Once data were collected, analyses followed four sequential steps:

1. Read for the sense of the whole.

2. Determine meaning units.

3. Transform participants' natural attitude expressions into phenomenologically sensitive expressions.

4. Determine the structure.

Briefly summarized, the method follows progressive refinement of each original description, as I initially did not do anything but read the

---

anonymity. This is unfortunate, but reflects traditional theological convictions rather than faulty sampling procedures. Because all participants are men, the masculine pronoun "he" is used throughout the study. References to God are also given in the masculine. Again, this reflects tradition, theological conviction, and the use among participants. See Gunnestad, "Kvinner i Lederskap"; and Smidsrød, "For Such a Time as This" for recent discussions on female leadership in the Norwegian Pentecostal movement.

40. Giorgi insists that at least three participants are required to ensure variation in the raw data, but notes trade-off between the amount of data collected per subject and the number of subjects included in a study. As a rule of thumb, the greater the amount of data gathered from each participant, the fewer participants are required. In contrast to statistical research, which makes claims about a population, phenomenological inquiry makes claims about a phenomenon. This being the case, sample size is not critical in phenomenology as sampling within this framework is about quality and depth, not size. See Englander, "Interview," 21–23; Todres, "Clarifying the Life-World," 109.

41. Giorgi spells out his method in several places; see, for instance, "Sketch of a Psychological Phenomenological Method"; *Descriptive Phenomenological Method*; or "Descriptive Phenomenological Psychological Method."

whole to get a grasp of the situated description. In the second step, each transcript was divided into meaning units, an analytical procedure based on my experience of transitions in meaning when the transcription is re-read from the beginning. These varied in length depending on the richness of the data in each passage. I then transformed the data into expressions that were more revelatory and sensitive to the phenomenon than the participant's everyday expressions, including terminology that is relevant for the discipline being utilized.[42] This third step, where the researcher tries to reach the essential meanings of the participant's experience through imaginative variation, is the heart of the method. Based on these transformed meanings, I described the structure of the phenomenon in a final step, addressed in chapter 5.

While providing the sequential steps which the researcher should follow in analyzing data, Giorgi's method is flexible, in the sense that the steps are implemented in a manner sensitive to the research situation. A slight modification in this project was to include individual structures as an analytical tool to summarize each participant's experience of Pentecostal leadership at a lower level of abstraction than the general structure suggested by Giorgi. While first described by Giorgi in his earlier works as situated structures,[43] this procedure is now advocated by other phenomenologists to focus thematically on essential features as they appear in individual examples.[44] These individual structures were included to ensure the integrity of each individual description, since entire interview transcripts were excluded for confidentiality reasons, and they were used together with the transformed meaning units to describe the general structure of Pentecostal leadership, and are presented prior to the general structure in chapter 5.

---

42. Appendix B illustrates the progress through steps 1–3. Due to the small size of the Norwegian Pentecostal movement, entire transcripts are not included in the study, as this would jeopardize the anonymity of the participants. Excerpts are thus provided to illustrate research method only.

43. Giorgi, "Convergence and Divergence"; Giorgi, "Sketch." Giorgi also acknowledges that this is a possible methodological step in his later writing; see Giorgi, "Theory, Practice, and Evaluation," 242.

44. de Castro, "Introduction"; Wertz, "Psychological Description"; Wertz, "Phenomenological Psychological Approach."

Concluding Remarks

This chapter outlines the method used in the phenomenological study, and argues for its rigor by pointing to the logical flow and consistency between philosophical assumptions, methodological considerations, and procedural steps.[45] Before describing the results of the study in the following chapter, it is useful to recapitulate what the phenomenological search for the essence of Pentecostal leadership does and does not set out to do.

The study does not aim to generate any theory of Pentecostal leadership. As highlighted by Giorgi, the goal of phenomenological inquiry is description, not theory development: "One motive for this strategy is that findings are more solid than theories, which, precisely because they are theories, always contain some speculative components."[46] This does not mean that the aim is merely to articulate individual experiences of the phenomenon. The descriptive phenomenological method is not primarily interested in the idiographic way in which the participant lived the phenomenon, but the general knowledge of it, implying a shift from particularities to a search for their common essence. This happens through imaginative variation where the phenomenon is varied freely in its possible forms. The empirical is important because essences only manifest themselves through experiences, but through free imaginative variation the phenomenologist goes beyond what is empirically given to detect an object's essence.[47] That which remains constant through the different variations, then, is considered the essence of the phenomenon.

However, one should not understand the essential structure as the full and final description of the phenomenon. Husserl held that essences allow possibilities for further exploration, meaning that they are never completely described but open and expandable.[48] Giorgi's understanding of essence as "a careful description of the structure of the lived experience of that phenomenon in a particular type of situation" reflects this notion.[49] Data collected elsewhere might have produced different results. It follows that the phenomenologist cannot claim that his findings have universal

---

45. See Appendix A for a longer discussion on how rigor is enhanced in the study.

46. Giorgi, "Concerning a Serious Misunderstanding," 56.

47. Zuesse, "Role of Intentionality."

48. Dahlberg, "Essence of Essences," 16.

49. Giorgi, "Concerning a Serious Misunderstanding," 41.

implications; the role of context is too critical.[50] Essences are never regarded as eternal, decontextualized, or Platonic truths, but as essences for a given intersubjective community.[51] However, the researcher might suggest that his findings have implications beyond the idiosyncratic and empirical. The descriptive phenomenological method is nomothetic in the sense that the meaning of a phenomenon has plausible generality to others who have experienced it.[52] In short, "the eidetic structure that is discovered and described is considered to be typical rather than universal,"[53] similar to the generalization that takes place in what sociologists have called the middle range.[54] With this in mind, attention is turned to the results of the phenomenological analysis.

50. Giorgi, "Phenomenological Movement," 78; Zuesse, "Role of Intentionality," 58.

51. Applebaum, "Beyond Scientism and Relativism," 44.

52. Englander, "Interview," 23.

53. Giorgi, "Husserl and Heidegger," 65.

54. Giorgi, *Descriptive Phenomenological Method*, 196.

5

A General Structure of
Pentecostal Leadership

THIS CHAPTER PRESENTS THE structure of participants' experiences of Pentecostal leadership, the fourth and final step in the descriptive phenomenological method. This structure describes the essence of Pentecostal leadership by explicating the constituents that make up the phenomenon. The notion of constituents is drawn from gestalt theories of perception, in which a gestalt is a structure that is different from, yet constituted by, the sum of its parts. As such, the structure is not a mere summation of parts, but is codetermined by the relationship between whole and part.[1] According to Giorgi,

> The structure of the experience is a way of understanding the unity of the concrete data. It is a way of understanding why diverse facts and concrete details can belong to the same phenomenon . . . The structure is the identification of the constituents that are essential for the phenomenon to manifest itself in this particular way as well as an understanding of how the constituents relate to each other.[2]

In other words, the structure is a second-order description of the raw data provided by the participants, detected by scanning the transformed meaning units (Step 3 in Giorgi's method) and the individual structures described below to decide whether their differences can be designated in one structure (infrastructural variations), or whether they are so large that two or several structures are necessary (interstructural variations). For the

1. Robbins, "Being Joyful," 188.
2. Giorgi, *Descriptive Phenomenological Method*, 200.

present study, one general structure was discovered as constituted by the relationship among eight constituents, meaning that it collapses if one of these are removed.

Prior to describing the general structure and elaborating on the empirical variations within each of the constituents below, the individual structures of the four participants are presented separately to illuminate how each individual experiences Pentecostal leadership. These individual structures are more situated than the general structure, as they are based on the experience of only one participant, hence remaining "more faithful to the concrete subject and specific situation whereas the general description . . . tries as much as possible to depart from the specifics to communicate the most general meaning of the phenomenon."[3] Thus, the individual structures are written to retain the concrete situations and moments of the original protocol, yet with an emphasis on the meaning of the experience as it relates to Pentecostal leadership, and with caution not to risk the anonymity of the participants. Since the project aims at inquiry into the experiences of Pentecostal leadership rather than the biographical stories of the participants, no narrative plot lines are identified from the interviews. Therefore, descriptions are episodic and focused on the phenomenon and its meaning rather than chronological presentations of events. In the subsequent explication of structure, the abbreviation P refers to an ideal participant. When referring to a specific research participant, he is identified as P1, P2, P3, or P4.

Individual Structures

Participant 1

When P1 started as a pastor, he was given the responsibility to develop a worship service aiming at spiritual seekers. He soon realized that there was discrepancy between the church's formal understanding of itself as a gathered community and the reality on the ground, since it had no unified sense or common purpose for the various worship services. In setting direction for the congregation, P1 chose a team of leaders based on their perceived potential to lead. Rather than waiting for divine revelation in solitude, then, P1 exercised his leadership based on the collective wisdom of the group, augmenting ownership and voluntarism in the organization by including others in leadership. While leadership was shared through empowerment

---

3. Giorgi, "Sketch," 20.

and delegated decision-making, P1 retained his influence by setting the agenda and defining the space within which decisions could be made.

P1's motivation to lead stems from a strong sense of commitment to God's mission in the world and a deep belief in the power of the biblical message to change people's lives. He refrains from using calling language because he thinks such terminology has so many connotations in Pentecostalism that he does not identify with. The church's mission and message are primary, and it was during the formative years of late adolescence that he came to believe that he could serve through leadership—and that it was possible to do so in a way that was authentic and sensible to an unbelieving world. He is suspicious of one-sided charismatic leaders who are not transparent about their own struggles and humanity, and seeks to model a life that is sustainable and a spirituality that is understandable. This involves his entire life—from family relations to how he stewards his money—because he perceives his leadership holistically as something he embodies rather than something he performs.

From the outset, the stress on keeping the congregation attentive to spiritual seekers has been a key aspect of P1's leadership. In setting direction for the church, he seeks to keep the biblical and spiritual content intact while freeing it from traditional cultural containers that makes it inaccessible or irrelevant for people who are not used to going to church. He thus describes his leadership in terms of a translator of religious meaning for unbelieving people. Further, he gives spiritual seekers a privileged position in evaluating organizational performance: when there are conflicting interests between long-time church goers and unchurched people—which in P1's experience happens rather often because believers are inclined to develop internal codes that exclude outsiders—he wants to draw attention to the concerns of those who do not believe. This attentive attitude toward outsiders is coupled with a pragmatic and utilitarian stance toward spirituality and methodology as a means to reach the higher organizational goals of reaching the lost and enhancing human flourishing. Forms and practices that do not support these aims are short-lived in P1's realm of influence.

This is not without conflict, however, since different people come to the congregation with different cultural and spiritual preferences and understandings. The Pentecostal organization is no blank slate, and it is P1's experience that leadership in it entails entering an ideological force field with contrasting views of ecclesiology and spirituality and, especially in his case, of how one should understand the Pentecostal tradition. Some ten years into his pastorate, P1 finds the hardest part of his leadership to be juggling the pressure of the Pentecostal heritage with the need to be understandable to the wider community. For P1, this tension is solved by adhering to an ambivalent and eclectic stance to the Pentecostal tradition, which he believes to entail a mixture of gold and garbage.

While P1 finds parts of the Pentecostal culture and spirituality problematic, he also finds it promising that it is a relatively young movement and thus open to impulses from other Christian traditions. Consequently, he advocates the implementation of cultural relevant practices over traditional Pentecostal spirituality when they are better fit to reach unbelievers. For P1, it is the role of the Pentecostal leader to sift through this spiritual reservoir to promote what he perceives to be good and hold back what is destructive for the development of the congregation.

Thus, P1 leads by shaping collective identity and spirituality, choosing on behalf of the congregation in situations where there were several options, thereby defining the goals and expressions of the Pentecostal congregation. This process may lead to a breakdown of leader relationships if the conflict line goes between various congregational leaders of different spiritual temperaments or preferences. P1 recalls how he put his foot down when a new pastor encouraged classic Pentecostal spirituality with spontaneous participation and free-floating use of the charismatic gifts in public gatherings because P1 sensed that it scared unchurched people. In deciding what to do in such incidents of leadership disagreement, P1 believes that solutions are found in conversations and processes where the strongest argument holds the upper hand.

While he understands his leadership to be derived, that he ultimately leads on behalf of God, he rarely experiences God speaking directly about what the church should do in different situations. Rather, his leadership involves the ongoing practice of prayer and surrender to discern what God is doing in both the culture and the congregation, yet this happens in a seamless connection between the spiritual and the rational where God's leading is most clearly detected in retrospect.

Participant 2

To hear, discern, and respond to God's will is pivotal to P2's experience of leadership in the Pentecostal congregation. For him, the overarching direction for his and the church's life is derived from divine revelation, making his leadership intuitive and spiritual throughout. While spirituality in this way is prominent in setting direction for the organization, it is not limited to certain tasks or aspects. On the contrary, P2 relies on spiritual sensitivity in all spheres and downplays the distinction between spiritual and practical by hearing from God as part of his leadership in both realms.

For P2, the emphasis on hearing God's voice in leadership does not undermine the role of human leaders. Quite the opposite—P2 experiences that leadership happens as an interplay between divine and human actors in which the leader's prime responsibility is to discern where God is leading the organization. It follows that hearing from God through spiritual disciplines is a pivotal aspect of leadership. P2 often experiences that God speaks to him directly and specifically about leadership initiatives or decisions, and he typically detects God's leading through a state of inner peace, confirmed by a Bible verse delivered by others or received in prayer and contemplation. This can happen in solitude, but it habitually involves a process of communal scrutiny and discernment with other leaders in the church.

Because divine revelation may take the organization in directions that are otherwise outside his agenda or horizon, P2's leadership includes elements of surprise when God discloses unforeseen aspects of his will. In this sense, P2's leadership is derived, as he leads on behalf of God. Also, P2's understanding of his leadership entails identification with the biblical narrative and characters in salvation history who were successfully led by God. Just as the Bible shows how many leaders among the people of God lacked the formal credentials necessary to take on such positions, P2 admits that his leadership team by the natural eye lacks the competence to lead the congregation. However, through collective competence in seeking and discerning God's will together, the organization thrives. For P2, this confirms that knowledge and proficiency is important but not critical for leadership in the Pentecostal organization—what is of uttermost importance is to be filled with the Holy Spirit.

While seeking God's will for the organization, P2 does not expect divine guidance and providence to automatically guarantee success. Rather, it is the responsibility of human leaders to find ways to put the overarching direction into practice through an ongoing process of discernment that certainly involves spiritual disciplines, but also human reasoning and pragmatic considerations. While God, at times, speaks very specifically to P2 about what the organization should do, there are other occurrences where the divine mandate comes in the form of a general invitation to enter a field of opportunities where leaders have great freedom to choose their way within God's will.

The notion that God opens doors for the church to enter generates confidence, and releases P2 and his coleaders to engage in innovation and entrepreneurship. Because God speaks, ecclesial leaders may go beyond conventional rationality to dare and endure things that would otherwise seem impossible. In this sense, the wider context is perceived in terms of its opportunities. The organization's relationship to its sociocultural environment is also difficult, however, and P2 describes how he finds it challenging to combine grace and truth, welcoming sinners yet confronting sin, in a non-Christian culture. In fact, P2 describes this balancing act between faithfulness to the normative Scripture and inclusion of people from secular backgrounds as one of the most difficult aspects of his leadership.

The experience of hearing God's voice and discovering God's way for the congregation not only gives P2 confidence to lead; it is also a means of influence in aligning corporate and democratic decision-making processes with what he perceives to be the divine will for the church. P2 narrates his experiences with God for the congregation, and uses them as an argument in seeking to convince others, thus pursuing others to follow his lead because he follows God. The confidence to do so stems from a profound sense of calling at the center of P2's understanding of himself as leader. With this calling comes assurance that God will be with him in everything he does, a security that P2 would not dare to lead without. While P2 seeks and expects observable and quantitative growth, success is ultimately understood in terms of faithfulness toward the divine calling.

P2 holds it to be crucial that the leader present his life as a model to emulate in order to move the organization in the looked-for direction. Positively, by sharing testimonies of how he experiences God's presence in his daily life, P2 builds confidence in his leadership among congregants and encourages them to trust God in their own lives. Negatively, P2 fears that his faults and failures might hinder the growth of the congregation. Either way, P2 holds Pentecostal leadership to be holistic and embodied because the shape of the leader's life impacts the development of the organization. Consequently, modeling of desired behaviors and narration of spiritual experiences and revelations are prime means of influence in P2's leadership.

Participant 3

P3 has been a leader in several Pentecostal congregations and points out the diversity between the different organizational settings. In his experience, Pentecostal leadership is no uniform phenomenon, but rather local and contextual as it takes on different forms in different organizations. Regardless of contexts, however, P3 understands leadership in terms of setting direction for the congregation. In doing so, he has the perspective of a gardener, one who sees the potential in each member and cultivates an environment in which people discover who they are and are empowered and released to contribute based on their natural and spiritual abilities. It follows that the leader should not only look for ways that people can serve his vision, but actively seek and listen to each member's genuine input and contribution to the vision of the church. The development of a shared leadership team is part of this process. The inclusion of numerous people in leadership, in turn, generates diversity that is held together through trustful relationships within the organization. As such, leadership involves the management of multiplicity within a common passion for the local church. In P3's experience, relational competence is crucial in this regard, because his leadership is not stronger than the relational bonds with members of the congregation.

In leading, P3 draws on the biblical narrative as understood through the lens of Pentecostal spirituality, and advocates access to the spiritual gifts as witnessed in the early church for himself and others. He admits that the relationship to the Pentecostal tradition is ambiguous, however. To define and model what Pentecostal spirituality and scriptural faithfulness looks like in the local congregation is, therefore, an important part of his leadership.

In P3's experience, God may lead him or the organization in directions that go outside or beyond the leader's agenda, understanding, or expectation. Intuition, openness for the unexpected, and respect for the unfinished, therefore, characterize his leadership. For P3, these intuitive and spiritual aspects of leadership must interact with cognition and human rationality. It is not either/or: P3 describes the seamless interaction between the two as a dance where both partners are necessary. If one aspect is ignored, diversity falters, leaving the congregation poorer than it is if differences in gifting, spirituality, and personality are allowed to coexist. This act of balancing strategy and pragmatism with spirituality and intuition is, for P3, difficult yet crucial for what it means to lead the Pentecostal congregation.

The multifaceted and undefined character of Pentecostal identity and spirituality leaves the leader in a constant stance of learning and emergence. In P3's experience, learning in Pentecostal contexts comes just as much through breaks and crisis as it does through linear, manageable, and cumulative processes. For instance, P3 describes how, in one church, he had to deal with toxic congregational meetings where some individuals used this arena to front their personal pet peeves. This was contrary to the trusting and empowering atmosphere P3 wanted in the church, and he thus had to rebuke some congregants to endorse a different culture and demonstrate acceptable organizational behavior. In doing so, he sometimes found himself acting contrary to the very culture he wanted to promote. In such instances, he felt that God corrected the way he treated congregational members, and thus compensated for the leadership training and mentoring he lacked during the first years of ministry. This took place in a period of much prayer, and highlights the role of spiritual disciplines in P3's leadership.

While P3 embraces previous experiences in terms of learning, he has also felt how Pentecostal leadership may come with a personal and professional price tag. P3's experience is that congregational change is no one way-street where the leader enters unexploited territory waiting to be molded by the pastor. On the contrary, each Pentecostal church has preferences and narratives that the leader must deal with and take into consideration if his leadership is to bear fruit. As P3 moved to pastor a new church, for example, he experienced that the very things that made him a good leader in one church gave him problems in the next. While he was able to bend the organizational discourse in one congregation, he was bent under its weight in another. In the new congregation, there were other expectations of the leader, and little match between P3's spirituality and strengths on one side and organizational demands on the other. Despite attempts to assemble a team of leaders with complementary gifts, P3 discovered that he was unable to meet the expectations the organization had to its prime leader, resulting in relational tensions and personal meltdown. While he understands leadership to be about setting the direction for the congregation, he painfully experienced that the organizational discourse frames the leader's ability to exercise leadership in it.

What has made P3 continue as a leader amidst the challenges he has faced in the congregation is a profound and continuous sense of calling—to ministry, in general, and to the church in which he serves, in particular.

P3 received a calling to the pastorate in his late childhood years, and this peak experience has shaped his life ever since. When turmoil surfaced in his leadership, then, the notion of being called to this specific vocation provided the bedrock of his personal and professional identity.

Participant 4

P4's description of Pentecostal leadership begins with his calling experience years before he entered pastoral ministry. During a time of seeking God for direction in his late adolescent years, he experienced how God revealed some very specific things he should do in his lifetime. His life and leadership have been shaped around this profound sense of being called and set aside by God for a specific purpose. The divine mandate becomes the reference point for everything P4 is and does, in private as well as in official roles.

With the sense of destiny comes faith to act and move toward the fulfillment of the vision. Thus, while P4's leadership begins with God taking initiative, it does not end there. P4 is a recipient before God, but he is also the helmsman and prime initiator before the congregation. Since God has spoken, the leader may speak and transform the will of God into the way of the organization, seeking to shape current realities in light of future fulfillments. This opens a space for innovation and entrepreneurship, and for using insights from leadership and management theory in combination with spiritual disciplines. In P4's description, then, successful leadership happens when the divine impulse meets an active and attentive human agent who is willing to submit to the Spirit's leading, even at the expense of his own reputation or comfort.

Since P4's leadership starts by listening to God, he understands it as received rather than claimed, derived rather than taken. In a profound sense, he leads on behalf of someone else. It follows that it is of uttermost importance for him to grasp and pursue God's will for his life and the church. His leadership relies on his ability to discern God's leading, the whereabouts of the congregation, and the challenges and opportunities of the wider context. As these change, so must the way he leads. This means that leadership plays out as an integrating and intuitive process—a polyphonic listening to the voices of God, church, and culture, one that involves spiritual and cognitive abilities in harmony.

P4's leadership is derived and as such, agenda and timing are not something P4 is entirely free to set, but rather must attend to. This sometimes leaves P4 in a tension where he is squeezed between organizational demands and the need to wait for the Spirit's leading. Spirituality may have a timing of its own, and it is important for P4 that organizational demands do not force the intuitive process, but rather augment it and adapt to it. This spiritual sensitivity must thus be allowed to permeate leadership across the organization, generating respect for the unfinished in the church as the people of the Spirit in which members share a language beyond the rational. Although the leader's central role in this process results in an asymmetrical relationship between leader and followers, hierarchy is modified by a collective spirituality and a culture of mutual respect and trust.

While P4's leadership is based upon his sense of being called and his ability to discern what God wants to do, it is sanctioned by the organization. Without trusting relationship with fellow workers, P4's ability to lead is floundering. Hence, P4's leadership happens in a reciprocal process in which the organization bolsters his influence by providing the space to seek God and empowering him to do so on their behalf. As such, leadership is, at least partially, attributed and coconstituted, and involves the leader's ability to discern God's will and make it meaningful and attainable for the organization. P4 acts as a transformer—not by deciding everything, but by framing the organizational discourse, defining what is central, and unfolding the vision for the church at a pace it can sustain.

P4 understands leadership as influence, and since this is not something he can turn on and off as he chooses, it underscores the totality and scope of his leadership; it is impossible to separate it from his life, as one cannot describe the former without the latter. P4's leadership begins in his heart from an inner center where he intuitively senses God's leading. To ensure that encounters with the divine may take place, P4 protects his inner, spiritual life from negative attitudes toward others and actively seeks God's guidance through prayer, solitude, and spiritual practices. As such, P4 is more than a passive medium or receiver of divine revelation; God's leading and P4's obedience are intertwined, and internal attitudes precede external leadership behaviors. What begins in the heart in turn spills over to the organization. His leadership flows out of his being and is holistic as he influences the church by presenting his life as a model to be emulated. This holistic perspective undermines a sacred/secular divide, as P4 rejects a dichotomy between the spiritual and material domains, but advocates a seamless interaction between the two. This frees the leader to draw from both spiritual and rational resources, to be prophetic yet pragmatic.

General Structure of Pentecostal Leadership Among Norwegian Pastors

For P, Pentecostal leadership is motivated by a sense of higher, divine purpose, a commitment to serve God's plans and purposes for the congregation and the world. As such, P views his leadership as derived from God, implying that he leads on behalf of someone else. Because P's God is active in the world, the leader's ability to discern what God says and does is essential, making spiritual practices crucial to P's leadership.

Although P must discern God's way and will, his leadership is not reduced to simply listening and obeying. Rather, the Pentecostal belief that God is active in every aspect of life frees P to overcome the sacred/secular divide and seamlessly combine spirituality and rationality in leading the organization. In doing so, P draws on the Pentecostal tradition in eclectic and often unsystematic ways, perceiving it as both resource and challenge, as something to be defined as much as defining for the organization. It is, therefore, up to P to set the direction for the Pentecostal congregation and define its reality, including its goals and spirituality, within the perimeters of the biblical narrative and God's overall guidance for the group. As his leadership rests on persuasion more than position, verbal communication is of key importance in this process.

P depends on the community's recognition of his leadership to be able to lead. As such, P's experience of leadership happens in a dialectic relationship between agency and structure, in which his ability to influence the organization hinges on his ability to adapt to the organization. It follows that P's leadership in the congregation is partly constituted and exercised in community with trusted others. Also, P leads the Pentecostal congregation in ways that take into consideration and adapt to the sociocultural context in which it is situated. In all of this, P leads the Pentecostal organization with his life, having modeling as a prime source of influence while seeking to integrate doing and being in a holistic leader identity.

Constituents and Empirical Variations

Motivated by a Sense of Higher, Divine Purpose

For P, the motivation to lead comes from a deep sense of commitment to serve God's plans and purposes for the congregation and the world. While all the participants hold this conviction, they experience it in empirically different ways. Three of the participants (P2, P3, and P4) express the motivation to enter ministry in terms of being called by God to this specific vocation. This sense of being called to lead the local congregation helps them overcome personal and organizational struggles and serves as the plumb line by which they evaluate their ministerial success. P3 and P4, specifically, described how a calling experience early in life was pivotal, not only for their future ministry but for the direction of their life.

> I was 11–12, out in the field playing with some cows or something. And I remember God saying to me in that moment, "When you grow up, you will be a pastor" . . . I didn't share that with anyone until I was done with high school. No parents, no one. But already then the course of my life was set. (P3)

For P4, calling grew out of an intense period of seeking God's will for his life in his adolescent years. During this period, he wrote down a list of priorities that has guided and shaped the direction of his life ever since. For all three participants, calling is not primarily a private, esoteric feeling, but a conviction and motivation to act today based on what God has said about what is to come. In this way, calling works proleptically by propelling them into action to shape present realities in light of future events. In P2's words, "I had never dared to enter the ministry [without it] . . . it assures me that God in a way will always be with me in what I said 'yes' to."

For P1, motivation to take on pastoral ministry in the Pentecostal congregation does not involve any specific calling to do so. In fact, he is resistant to use calling phraseology to describe his way into ministry due to the connotations the term has in Pentecostal circles. Rather than a personal calling experience, then, his leadership grew out of a commitment to the truthfulness of the Christian message and a desire to serve it with his life. During a spiritual formative period in his late teenage years, he experienced leadership in a way that was explicitly Christian yet relevant to his unbelieving friends. "That did something to me. Both my confidence in being a leader and the possibility of being a Christian leader without being a nitwit" (P1). Since a calling experience was absent in P1's life and leadership, his commitment goes more directly with the message for which he is a messenger. "It is a message I too cling to. But the message is powerful; I believe in it" (P1).

For all participants, commitment to the divine purpose equals commitment to the biblical narrative as a normative script for the church and its leaders. This is more than a cognitive affirmation of certain beliefs; the notion of a higher, divine purpose involves personal identification with the biblical narrative and an understanding of leadership as taking part in the outworking of God's purposes for the church and the world. Being called to ecclesial leadership thus means being called to see one's life as grafted into the biblical narrative. As P2 states,

> The calling [has] guaranteed that God is with us but also the assurance that . . . there is a solution, a victory, in that which God called us into—just as he fulfilled it for the all characters in the Bible.

In short, the participants hold that their role as leaders involves defining and setting direction for the congregation. This does not mean that their leadership stems from or even starts with them taking the initiative. On the contrary, it begins in submission to a cause beyond themselves and is fueled by the energy from an encounter with the divine.

Derived Leadership

Closely related to the previous constituent, P views his leadership as derived from God, implying that he leads on behalf of someone else. Because P's God is active in the world, the leader's ability to discern what God says and does is essential, making spiritual practices crucial in P's leadership. P1 epitomizes this point in describing how he typically starts meetings by turning to God in prayer:

> We can look back and over time see that God was with us. We were led, there was a hand over us—and I surrender to that hand. That's why I almost always pray, "God, once again I surrender into your hands. Once again we surrender into your hands." There is a dimension of surrender in leadership, then. That I lead on behalf of.

P4 expresses the same idea when he describes how he must wait for God's directions when leading the organization. Since God is the ultimate leader, P4 and his fellow workers must respect the Spirit's timing and not push premature decisions to meet organizational demands. Instead, they must cooperate in nourishing a culture that supports and promotes the spiritual sensitivity of the leader: "We must respect the pastor's inner clock. Things will be good in the end, but we do not always decide the timing" (P4). This unpredictable factor in P4's leadership means that the organization must learn to handle a state of liquidity, of not always seeing as far ahead as it would like to. Because leadership is derived and rests on the leader's ability to discern God's will, P4 describes how he protects his heart from wrong attitudes toward others and finds a peaceful place, preferably in the morning, to hear what God is saying when making major decisions. The idea of peace is also evident in P2's description of Pentecostal leadership. He mentions several examples of how God, often quite surprisingly for P2, gives specific directions about what the organization should do in spiritual as well as practical matters. For P2, assurance of what is God is up to typically comes through prayer, an inner sense of peace, and a Bible verse that provides direction in the present situation.

The practice of constantly turning one's attention to God as part of their leadership is essential to all the participants, not only in extraordinary situations but habitually in the daily routines of organizational work. P1 admits that he is not the most active in prayer nights or long prayer meetings, yet highlights the critical role of prayer in his leadership, saying, "It is extremely important to me . . . because I experience it as tuning in [to God]." While P1 rarely receives detailed instructions from God in how he should lead the congregation, some of the others occasionally do. P3 recounts a situation where he was new in the congregation and felt lonely in the process of changing a toxic church culture. With little human support, he spent much time in prayer and perceived how God not only helped him lead the church, but shaped him in the process. "I experienced God as my mentor. And it got really specific. I didn't only sense a presence; I got thoughts, ideas, I got corrections, I was rebuked" (P3). In sum, there are empirical variations in how the participants discern where God is leading the congregation, but they are unison in the understanding of leading on behalf of God. They are serving a purpose beyond themselves, and their leadership is ultimately derived from this mission.

Human and Divine Agency in a Seamless Interaction Between Rationality and Spirituality

Although the leader must discern God's way and will, P's leadership is not reduced to simply listen and obey. The examples above may give the impression that the leader is a marionette destined to execute the divine will. In reality, the picture is much more complex. The Pentecostal leader is no monarch, but he is certainly more than a mouthpiece. More often than not, the idea of being led by God liberates rather than limits P to proactively engage in organizational matters. Specifically, the Pentecostal belief that God is active in every aspect of life frees P to overcome a sacred/secular divide and seamlessly combine spirituality and rationality in leading the organization. For example, P4 describes the relationship between the human and the divine in how he seeks to realize the calling from God by means of tools and techniques from conventional leadership thinking:

> What I have received faith for, are my life goals. It's like God has put faith for it in my heart. Then I use, in my daily work, skills like communication, administration, leader[ship]—things like that. But it is because I have faith in the destination to which I am headed that I work here and now.

This brief statement epitomizes the interplay between spirituality and rationality, primitivism and pragmatism, in Pentecostal leadership. Because God has acted, the leader is free to act. Also, it confirms a point made earlier, namely that the leader's sense of destiny works proleptically; the human leader actively shapes the future according to the divine mandate, rather than passively waiting for it to be fulfilled. Put differently, the future provides the lens that focuses energy in the present.

One distinct area in which the participants differed significantly in regard to the interaction between human and divine agency relates to the openness for intuition and surprise in leadership. P1 allows for but is skeptical of processes where a direct word from God settled the issue: "We have not made any leadership decisions where someone states 'so says the Lord.' To me, that would be strange." Rather than relying on intuition and spiritual sensibility, he describes a culture of finding a way through collective reasoning. "We gather around a table and talk, and the strongest idea wins through" (P1). One should not overstate the dichotomy between spirituality and rationality here, given P1's emphasis on surrendering to God in prayer; yet to him, God's leading is more clearly detected in retrospect than as a direct intervention in leadership processes.

On the other side of the spectrum, P2 frequently experiences how God speaks directly and concretely about what the leaders should do. He recounts an incident when he was driving out of a parking lot after work when God spoke two words out of the blue—"buy building"—about a property near the church. He was perplexed by what this meant, but the following morning a prayer leader in the church testified that God had spoken two words one night: "buy building." This and a confirming verse from the Bible assured him and the leadership team to invest in the actual building. This incident is not unique; P2 points to numerous occurrences where God has spoken very specifically to him about things that he or the church should do—also in ways that were surprising and not on his radar. On other occasions, the divine mandate takes the form of a general authorization, an incitement to move in a certain direction, while leaving much room for human creativity and freedom in implementing it. The notion that leadership is derived and leaders must discern what God is up to for the congregation and its context, therefore, does not then hinder P from taking initiative and making strategies. On the contrary, that God is actively unfolding his plan and changing lives and societies releases leaders to act with confidence and creativity. Because God speaks, the leader may go beyond conventional rationality to dare and endure things that would otherwise seem impossible. In P2's experience, ecclesial leaders are never reduced to mere finger puppets in the divine drama, but hold status as agents who actively seek opportunities in their surroundings.

> I sensed very strongly that the Lord said, "many doors will open for you from this time on, and you can choose to only peek into the room and go on. But if you choose to enter when I have opened the door, it is in reality the same promise spoken to Joshua, that I will give you every place where you set your foot." So, with this general revelation as a backdrop, we have been very attentive to doors that have been opened. (P2)

The sense of divine guidance and providence does not automatically guarantee success. Rather, P2 holds that it was the responsibility of the leaders to find ways to put the overarching direction into practice through an ongoing process of discernment by means of spiritual disciplines, human reasoning, and pragmatic considerations. As such, human agency is not oppositional to but instead a part of the outworking of God's purpose for the organization. In P2's words,

> I often say that it is like steering a boat; you can't just set the rudder and go to sleep. You must constantly correct for winds and currents. And that's how I feel about leadership: We must sit at the wheel of the ship all the time.

Though contrasting in how they detect God's leading, the differences between P1 and P2 demonstrate the common theme of interplay between action and discernment, human and divine agency, in Pentecostal leadership.

The descriptions show that spirituality is prominent in setting direction for the organization and not limited to certain tasks or aspects, meaning that the distinction between spiritual and practical is downplayed since P hears from God as part of his leadership in both realms. How spirituality and rationality integrate into actual leadership differs among the participants. Diverging views on the use of the spiritual gifts in worship services illustrate this point. The greatest tension here is between P1 and P3, the former being rather skeptical to charismatic utterings in public gatherings due to the negative effects they often have, in his experience, on spiritual seekers who are not familiar with the Pentecostal church culture:

> We must practice the charismatic gifts in such a way that what God wants to say in that room, if it should be uttered—with a big "if," then—if it should be uttered in the large setting, . . . it must be communicated in a way that makes sense to as many people as possible. (P1)

This emphasis frequently brings him in conflict with traditional Pentecostal understandings of spirituality emphasizing spontaneity and surprise, which in P1's view are so entrenched in tribal codes and language that they are a stumbling block rather than stepping stone in reaching out to an unbelieving world. Raw Pentecostal spirituality does not make sense to outsiders, and he thus takes on a mediating role in leading the congregation:

> And here I sometimes stand as a translator. On one side, I have the very internal Pentecostal people, and then I have the city and the unbelievers and our friends. And then I must hold back and say [to the first group] that it's not the God who burns in you I want to reject. I just want us to use a language that makes it possible for these [in the other group] to hear what you say. (P1)

While P3 by no means neglects the importance of relevance and understanding, he disagrees with P1's strict regime in controlling the use of spiritual gifts. "The God-factor, where the Spirit actually may surprise us a bit, we must allow room for that. Because it enriches the room with something unique, divine" (P3). Thus, P3 argues for a freer and more spontaneous use of the charismatic gifts in public gatherings than does P1—one in which "there is not only delivered a monologue aimed at reflection but a space for experience. There is now the experience of God here. Now we have time to allow people to actually taste something" (P3).

The role of Pentecostal spirituality and tradition is discussed more thoroughly in the next section. The point here is that, although Pentecostal leadership entails seamless shifts between spirituality and human reasoning, it is not free of tension. Spirituality, at least the Pentecostal version, may at times conflict with conventional thinking and rationality. Among the participants involved in the study, P1 most strongly tones down the intuitive side of Pentecostal leadership. This might be because he gives unbelievers such a privileged hermeneutical position in emphasizing their understanding as a yardstick of ministerial success. While the participants put different emphasis on intuition in their leadership, however, they all seek to balance spiritual discernment and rational cognition in their leadership. In P3's words,

> We must allow ourselves to trust our cognitive learning processes. We get smarter, we understand more. But they can never replace the guidance of the Spirit, which dances with cognition. The spiritual and the cognitive must go together. Then, I believe, we get the best. And Pentecostals at their best live in the dance between the two.

The Pentecostal genius, then, according to P3, is exactly the seamless interaction between spirituality and rationality, intuition and cognition, described as a dynamic dance between to competent partners. It is an ongoing process, rather than a static equilibrium, in which both apparatuses are engaged to find the will of God and the way of the church. It is not always an easy one, however: "The one is not better or worse than the other—it's just that they have to dance together. The question is whether they dance to the same melody. And who's going to lead? So, that's part of our challenge" (P3). While relying on organizational leadership skills in leading the congregation, P4 expresses the same concern when he describes the role of spirituality in ecclesial leadership:

> I believe in the Holy Spirit's identity as my guide, as my defender, as the one who leads me. That he's like a wind, he's like a wave— and that this is a vital part of reality. That it's just as real as the factual knowledge I have gained through accumulation of knowledge, experience, and reflection. Both dimensions are just as real, but . . . the guidance of the Spirit holds the highest authority. And for me, this is a place where I must surrender to a sort of naivety, in a way. For I have to trust in God's voice.

To sum up, for P, spirituality is not limited to the spiritual realm only, but has implications for all aspects of Pentecostal leadership. However, the integration of intuition and cognition in setting the direction for the Pentecostal congregation does not follow a predictable linear pattern, but happens in seamless—and at times conflicting—interaction between divine and human agency. The role of spirituality (especially spirituality in a Pentecostal key) in leadership is hence not settled, but remains an open discussion—as witnessed in the unpacking of the next constituent.

Pragmatic and Eclectic Stance Toward
the Pentecostal Tradition

In seeking to lead the congregation, P draws on the Pentecostal tradition in eclectic and often unsystematic ways. Rather than a uniform norm to which he must faithfully adhere, P approaches Pentecostal spirituality as a dynamic reservoir, as both resource and challenge, as something to be defined as much as defining. Starting with the latter, P1 describes "the old-fashioned Pentecostal paradigm," with its emphasis on charismatic utterings, spontaneous participation, end-time hysteria, and anti-ecumenical attitudes as problematic for many reasons, particularly because it is irrelevant and inaccessible for outsiders:

> In my view, everyone who has been a Christian for more than 45 minutes starts to develop peculiar interests, often in direct opposition to the needs of people who are seekers, not yet Christians. Hence, there is an ongoing battle for me as a pastor to keep the church open for newcomers.

As a consequence, he holds an ambivalent attitude toward his own Pentecostal tradition, adhering to the initial egalitarian ideal modelled by Seymour in the Azusa Street revival, yet admitting that this ideal was never realized in the subsequent Pentecostal history. For P1, then, the Pentecostal tradition consists of both gold and garbage, one from which he is free to draw or discard. Consequently, he advocates an eclectic stance toward it. "Our privilege as a young church[—]*de facto* we are a young church in a two-thousand-years-old history—the privilege is that we can be flexible in learning and using from other traditions" (P1). To do so is not optional, but mandatory. For P1, it is the duty of every Pentecostal leader to scrutinize the tradition to pass on what he perceives to be good and leave behind the clutter—a task that has not been properly addressed by previous leaders:

> I think that Pentecostal leaders two generations before me lacked the courage to do what the Pentecostal movement by its very nature does, namely to ask the question: What is God doing in our time? What does the Spirit say to the churches? They saw themselves merely as defenders [of the tradition].

While P1 is most outspoken in his critique of traditional Pentecostalism in Norway, none of the other participants adhere to some canon of Pentecostal orthodoxy. To do so would be absurd given the diversity within the movement. What is at stake, according to P3, is to define congregational spirituality:

> We must take ownership of our spirituality. . . . Because the Pentecostal movement, its voice is not unified. It is not homogeneous at all. You cannot retrieve it from somewhere because it is nowhere. It is highly subjective; therefore, we must take a subjective responsibility to define our spirituality and say, "this is how we believe it can be managed in a healthy, building, and correct way."

This, states P3, is an ongoing process of innovation and discovery, of taking hold of the Pentecostal ethos, yet in a manner that is theologically faithful and organizationally meaningful. This is challenging, as the members of the congregation have their own understandings and preferences of what it means to be a Pentecostal church. For instance, P3 experienced that more spiritually wired people fell short in cognitive decision-making processes: "Many of the charismatic, more intuitive gifts struggled to be heard. People with the best verbal skills won the discussions. Those who were not so clever at verbalization fell through." While P1 gives spiritual seekers a privileged position by emphasizing their perception of the church in shaping congregational spirituality, P3 laments this strategic way of managing spirituality because it alienates many of its members: "There is a good chunk of the congregation who is not comfortable with the very strategic, business-like. After all, the church is complex." P1 admits that sifting through the Pentecostal heritage is one of the most difficult parts of his leadership, as he constantly must juggle the pressure from the tradition with the need to be understandable to the wider community:

> It is not friction free. But, I believe, [there] are times when I must show that kind of leadership to reach where we want to go. And, therefore, my toughest fights in the job is not against the unchurched . . . My difficult battle is to hold back those [in the church] who want, "oh, now we need more of the traditional."

The underlying problem, then, is who gets to define valid and invalid spiritual expressions in the Pentecostal congregation. This is a delicate question, one where the leader may be perceived as limiting or controlling God. According to P1, the way to overcome this problem is to demonstrate and celebrate a spirituality that takes both God's presence and the need for order into consideration.

Though differently emphasized among the participants, a common goal for all is to transpose the authentic content of Pentecostal spirituality without its cultural container. For example, P4 describes how he, like classical Pentecostals, believes in and operates in the charismatic gifts. Different from his spiritual forefathers, however, he seeks to integrate the spiritual and human in a seamless whole—as discussed more fully in the previous section:

> Unlike old Pentecostals, I do not announce . . . "now comes a word of knowledge" or "now comes a prophecy." Paul says, "I pray continually"—it's like we touch upon a different, invisible film all the time, in our conversations and in our thoughts. More and more I want to make a seamless connection, because I don't want a dichotomy. I want one world and one reality, without being spooked.

As alluded to previously, the plasticity of the Pentecostal tradition opens doors for innovation and entrepreneurship. P2 describes how the leadership team was convinced through a series of divine oracles that they should not look back to see what would happen in the future. On the contrary, they sensed that God opened doors for them so that they could be innovative in areas that traditionally fall outside the scope of ecclesial engagement.

> The revival should come in a different manner than it had before, and there were no historical references in our own history—or maybe not in the history of the Norwegian Pentecostal movement either. And that has made the leadership very attentive to how we may be challenged in areas where no churches are currently engaged, yet where God is opening doors for us.

If the Pentecostal tradition is a resource more than a source, a wide array of opportunities opens for the Pentecostal leader. However, without the boundaries provided by tradition, there is always the risk that Pentecostal leadership not only ends up being seamless, but also borderless. In this regard, the participants describe the pragmatic, even utilitarian, tendencies in Pentecostal leadership. Subtly, P2's assurance that ministerial success confirms the divine mandate illustrates this attitude. More explicitly, P1 states,

> In our tradition, for good and for bad, that which works draws the attention. . . . Pentecostals typically say, "if it works, it is probably biblical." There is a weakness here, of course, I realize that, but there is something about having little tolerance for continuing with things that don't work over time.

P4 suggests that this utilitarian accentuation of results is especially prevalent in what he describes as an "entrepreneurial paradigm" among younger church planters in Norwegian Pentecostalism. While effective in terms of results, P4 fears that this pragmatism may draw backlash in the long haul, saying,

> I believe that the greatest challenge—at least among the circle of entrepreneurial leaders—is that things must work all the time to be legitimate. There must be some fruit here, it must function, it must create something. And if one is not able to reflect theologically about qualities but only deals with quantities, I believe that one soon will be exhausted as leader, soon be used up by the church and the environment, and soon be a slave of one's own vision.

In summing up, it seems clear that the eclectic and pragmatic stance toward the Pentecostal tradition is a two-edged sword. On one side, it fosters innovation by freeing leaders to actively choose the forms and methods that are best suited to serve the overall purpose of church in the time and place they exists. On the other side, the freedom from binding traditions may end up as a slippery slope of uncritical utilitarian emphasis on visible success. It seems this is an inherent tension in Pentecostal leadership.

Persuasive Communication

P sets the direction for the Pentecostal congregation within the parameters of the biblical narrative and God's overall guidance for the group. As his leadership rests on persuasion more than position, verbal communication is of key importance in this process. While there is shared emphasis on communication in the group, it plays out differently among the participants. P1 highlights preaching as a key aspect of his leadership in the Pentecostal congregation: "I lead primarily through leaders and as a preacher. And preaching is to me the most important arena." Though important, preaching comes at a price because of the laborious and time-consuming work of sermon preparation. Due to the emphasis on making the public meetings accessible to people who are not familiar with church culture, P1 stresses that sermons—as well as other elements of the worship service—should have high standards of quality and be relevant for the attendees. "Through preaching we highlight ideals . . . The sermon [must] be by the Word of God, but it must also be so specific that people know what to do with it. 'How do I live with this?'" (P1). P1's understanding of himself as an interpreter or translator of Pentecostal spirituality mentioned above belongs to this picture.

Among the other participants, P4 most strongly endorses P1's accentuation of preaching: "To preach sound and clear on Sundays and teach well in the various teaching opportunities that are given to me—that's my arena for leadership." Obviously, verbal communication is not the panacea of Pentecostal leadership; P4 sees public speaking in line with the more relational work of following up fellow leaders and caring pastorally for the congregation. Yet, in the voluntary Pentecostal organization, the communication of a compelling message and vision is important.

Persuasion through verbal communication is also evident in P2's description of Pentecostal leadership. In the democratic Pentecostal organization, leaders do not make decisions alone. Yet, by narrating how God has directed the leaders in the process leading up to communal decision-making meetings, they influence the congregation to respond in certain ways to the questions at hand. In the specific case of buying a building cited above, P2 described how he framed the called-for decision within his own experience of God's leading:

> I go to the congregation meeting and say it just as it is, tell them the greetings [from God] about buying building and the Bible verse [about God's providence if they decide to acquire the property]. And ask for their trust so that we can initiate the process of purchasing the building.

Thus, the divine initiative sensed by the leader is transformed into social influence through the communication of a convincing narrative where God and the leaders are key characters. P3's experience of Pentecostal leadership likewise includes examples of communication as a tool of influence and culture building in the congregation. What is particularly interesting in his description, however, is that this communication does not take place in vacuum. Rather, setting direction through communication often means getting involved in a rhetorical battle, a clash of competing narratives. P3 describes how, in one church, he had to quiet down informal leaders who used congregation meetings to advocate their personal agenda:

That is leadership, because you must set direction and you must say that we don't want this culture anymore. "You're not allowed to do this." And this is demanding for a [young pastor] who just moved to town, while he is [much older] and has a position and everyone knows him.

In another congregation, P3 experienced that spiritually wired people fell short in decision-making processes because their capabilities were not primarily in the area of communication: "Many of the charismatic, more intuitive gifts struggled to be heard. People with the best verbal skills won the discussions. Those who were not so clever at verbalization fell through." On the backside of effective leadership communication, then, are those whose voices were ignored or muted in the struggle for influence. While persuasive communication is important in Pentecostal leadership, not all communication is equally persuasive; not any argument will prevail. It is not only that leaders rely on verbal communication to shape the organizational discourse; they are also shaped by it. This complex relationship is addressed next.

Dialectic Relationship Between Structure and Agency

For P, leadership entails setting the direction for the congregation and defining its reality, including its goals and spirituality. At the same time, P depends on the community's recognition of his leadership to be able to lead. As such, P experiences leadership as happening in a dialectic relationship between agency and structure in which his ability to influence the organization depends on his ability to adapt to the organization.[4] It follows that P's leadership, to some extent, is constituted and exercised in community with trusted others.

A brief justification is necessary before the empirical variations of this constituent is explicated. The relationship between structure and agency—of influencing the organization, yet being influenced by it—is so embedded in organizational practices that it can be separated from the flow

4. I am aware that the terminology used here is theoretically loaded; yet, it is outside the scope of this study to discuss the use of the terms in the social sciences. What I am trying to address is the tension or opposition between two interacting forces in the Pentecostal congregation. Here "structure" refers to the institutional or systemic composition of relatively enduring features that make up the backdrop against which organizational life is carried out. "Agency" is the potential to resist, manipulate, or create these structural conditions for social existence (Parker, *Structuration*, 7).

of leadership descriptions for analytical purposes only. Arguably, it is no constituent of its own, but rather a latent tension in the others. The purpose of addressing it specifically, however, is to draw attention to the subtle yet important interplay between the individual and the collective in religious leadership.

In the previous section, P1 described how he feels free to draw from various ecclesial traditions rather than sticking rigidly to classic Pentecostal expressions in leading the congregation. Since there is no binding tradition in any substantial sense, the Pentecostal leader is an agent who plays a prominent role in shaping collective identity and spirituality by actively choosing on behalf of the congregation in situations where there were several options, thereby defining the goals and expressions of the Pentecostal organization. When it comes to the use of spiritual gifts in the worship service, for instance, P1 shapes the gathering in a way that he believes is faithful to the biblical intent and content, but relevant to people who are not familiar with the traditional Pentecostal altar call: "We believe in intercession by laying of hands; the Bible is quite clear on that point. But the Bible does not say that one must be ministered to in front of . . . one's friends." Spirituality is, according to this perspective, to some extent a dimension of ecclesial life that can be managed by leaders. In P1's description, this understanding manifests itself in a perceived distinction between form and content, paired with the implicit belief that one can change the former without influencing the latter. Church leadership is thus able to manage organizational spirituality in a manner that is better fit to meet the overall goal of reaching unchurched people than was the case with the traditional Pentecostal worship service.

> And I lead in this, in the sense that we run a process addressing why and how, and there is no strong counterforce against these changes. For there is no strong, conscious thought about how things were done the old way. That's why the new gains ground, because it has a clearer purpose. (P1)

When another leader tried to implement a traditional Pentecostal service with altar calls and intercession in front of the congregation, the influence of structure surfaced: "It worked very poorly. People found it awkward, people found it strange to go to the front, visible to all in this manner" (P1). Thus, while the leader has space to act as an agent of change due to the inherent flexibility in the Pentecostal tradition, the room of possibilities is not without restraints. If he goes beyond what the organization or other leaders deem appropriate or desirable, his influence may soon vaporize.

P3 learned this the hard way. Having experienced success in ministry by renewing a traditional Pentecostal church, he moved to another place to pastor a larger congregation. He soon realized that what he had excelled at in the first church was close to useless in the latter.

> Everyone up to this point, until I came here [to this church], always included me in strategy processes because I was the one who had a picture of the future, and I ended up making structures and leading. Here I felt like a jerk. I felt like a nobody, in this room and in this church, this leadership.

P3 described how his personality, gifting, and spirituality clashed with the expectations and leadership culture in the new church he was supposed to lead. Once a successful change agent in one setting, he was crushed under the burden of structure and expectancy in another. P3 is intuitively wired and has built the platform for his leadership on relational ties. In the new organizational domain, he sensed the demands for a CEO-pastor, a role that he was neither equipped for nor felt comfortable with taking on. He tried to assemble a team with complementary gifts, but discovered that he was unable to hold the diverse team together, resulting in relational tensions and personal meltdown.

> I shall now deliver, in the corporation . . . and all the things that I really burn for, I don't even have time or energy to attend. Because now I have to do all these other things. And this goes over time. And in the end, I not only have little confidence in myself; it starts affecting my self-esteem. I experience that I am not good enough. (P3)

The story illustrates that the leader is far from free to do whatever he pleases; if he wants to maintain influence, he must stay within the often implicit expectations the organization has for its leaders. In P3's experience, Pentecostal leadership is like entering a force field formed by personal and collective histories, experiences, and spiritualities. In all of this, leadership is emerging as the leader is trusted and granted influence when he meets the expectations of the organization. As such, leadership rests not merely (or even primarily?) on the leader's positional power, but on his ability to define and articulate reality and purpose in a way that is meaningful for members and co-leaders in the congregation. Leadership is hence a dynamic process of influence between leaders and organization, all framed by the ongoing narrative that shapes the organization's self-understanding in time and space. When the leader's right to define reality is disputed, there is a clash of narratives where contrasting sets of values and priorities compete for the soul of the congregation, resulting in antagonistic leadership patterns in which the leader may lose himself to win the congregation. In short, the leader is no isolated actor, but must adapt to the organizational structure and discourse to be able to lead.

From a different angle, the connection between structure and agency surfaces when P2 describes the relationship between leaders and congregation in terms of trust. While this leader, more so than the others, highlights how God leads the church directly through the charismatic gifts, he describes a reciprocal relationship between leaders and organization in following God's leading:

> When I use [the phrase] "God has spoken," I know that in its worst form it may sound like manipulation, but I dare to say that our experiences indicate that the church have confidence in what we do. It is not that all the prophetic has been fulfilled, . . . but I can't remember that we really failed by being way off or totally wrong. (P2)

Repeated success builds trust in the congregation, and this in turn bolsters the leaders' confidence and influence to lead the congregation. Further, influence is not limited to positional leaders, but described as a shared enterprise where everyone, at least in principle, is allowed to partake in leading the church because of the democratic distribution of spiritual gifts. P2 recalls a situation where several ordinary church members outside formal leadership roles felt that God called the church to take on certain responsibilities, an initiative that the leadership team later supported. In other incidents, P2 turns down requests about what he or the church should do:

> I try to be careful about the requests I get, to say yes to the things where I think that God might be involved. But if people come . . . with a mission like "now the church has to do something about this, right?" then they typically should start doing something about it themselves.

In practice, then, not every voice carries equal weight, and positional leaders function as gatekeepers in deciding which input and agenda should have priority in the organization. While P2's organization formally has a democratic structure, with the congregational meeting as the final decision-making body, he and the other leaders frame the organizational discourse and interpret events, and thereby define reality for the congregation. Wh involvement is encouraged at all levels, the team of elected leaders is responsible for setting the overall direction of the church and protecting this from other agendas in the organization. Thus, there are democratic and hierarchical forces at work simultaneously, leaving a paradoxical relationship between asymmetry and symmetry, pragmatism and spirituality, planning and spontaneity. Trust based on relationships and proven success in the past keeps this tension in balance and contributes to a sense of "we" in the organization.

The relationship between structure and agency looks empirically different in P4's experience, yet the same tension is present. In his description, P4 clearly acts as an agent in the organization by being the prime initiator and carrier of its vision: "That which flows from the leadership's values and priorities becomes celebrated in the organization. Those who take initiatives . . . on the fringes of this main stream, will have a harder struggle" (P4). Yet, the leader is not acting as an agent independent from the organization. On the contrary, there is a structure of support that enables P4 to find God's will for the organization:

> I have a social contract with my closest co-workers concerning deadlines. If we come to a point where I sense [that] the Lord doesn't say anything, I don't see it clearly, then I am allowed to say so. My closest colleagues cooperate with this spiritual sensitivity.

In summary, P's leadership does not exist in isolation, but is partly constituted by the community in which it takes place. Put differently, Pentecostal leadership happens in the interaction between agency and structure, and is effective when the leader manages to change or challenge existing thinking or practice without exceeding it completely. That the leader's ability to lead is also moderated by contextual factors is addressed in the next section.

Adaptive to Context

Closely related to the previous constituent, P leads the Pentecostal congregation in ways that take into consideration and adapt to the sociocultural context in which it is situated. Context is perceived as both problem and opportunity. In terms of the former, P2 expressed that the task of leading a religious organization in a secular environment was one of the greatest challenges in his leadership.

> How shall we as a church relate to the . . . moral deprivation that characterizes our nation? . . . How can we extend grace to everyone who needs it, while at the same time communicate the truth? I find it challenging to live in this [tension].

In a similar vein, P1 recognizes the cultural gap between the Pentecostal congregation and the wider society, but takes a more optimistic approach by emphasizing how cultural trends serve as resources that the church may draw upon in implementing culturally relevant spiritual practices:

> Lighting candles as a symbolic act is something that we don't have much tradition for, but one that is very available in the culture at the moment. After July 22th [date of terror attack in 2011], shops in the city went out of candles because so many people wanted to light one. So, we light candles [in worship services].

This inclusion of confessionally foreign, yet culturally appropriate, expressions of spirituality reflects the pragmatic stance toward tradition highlighted above and epitomizes P1's understanding of himself as a translator and interpreter of religious meaning to an unbelieving audience. In a similar vein, P4 notes how the national context and sentiment shapes his leadership. In setting direction for the church, for instance, he tries to adapt to Norwegian culture:

> No one in Norway is ignited by extreme ideas. You know, we have never landed on the moon. We have not taken over other nations since the Vikings were here a thousand years ago. The Norwegian sentiment is not [like] America. And it has been important for me to understand that.

Consequently, P4 unfolds the vision for the church in a pace it could sustain by not always communicating long-term goals, but rather action points that are achievable within reasonable time.

> There is an element of pragmatism in this. . . . Others may think that I am too obsessed with culture, but for me it is [a question of] cultural analysis. There is simply realism in the fact that if you don't deliver on subgoals in your vision, you should not talk too much about what you plan to do in the long haul. . . . Leaders in Norway don't have more leadership than the trust they have [earned].

Pentecostal leaders must not only deal with national culture, but also adjust to congregational culture in order to be effective. This is perhaps most evident in P3's experience of succeeding in one congregation and failing in another, as pointed out above. Despite the empirical differences between the participants' experiences, though, they all witness to how Pentecostal leadership in one way or another relates to the environment in which it takes place—be it congregational, local, or national context. Since Pentecostal identity and spirituality take on various forms in various congregations, Pentecostal leadership is a multifaceted phenomenon that looks empirically differently from context to context, leaving the leader in a constant stance of tension and learning.

Involving the Leader's Entire Life

P leads the Pentecostal organization with his life, modeling being a prime source of influence. He experiences his leadership as all-inclusive and seeks to integrate doing and being in a holistic leader identity. In this area, the univocal assertion of the all-embracing character of Pentecostal leadership overshadows the empirical variations among the participants. First, leadership involves modeling; the leader must walk the talk and exemplify what he wants to see in the organization. This spans from being open and authentic about one's imperfection and handling conflict in a Christ-like manner to demonstrating what kind of spirituality the leadership encourages in public worship services. In P3's experience,

> What happens in the large setting is the showcase of the church we build. So how can it happen in the smaller settings if we don't do anything or model it in the large gathering? We must model it for them to understand that it is important. If not, we say that it is not important.

According to P2, even the effective proclamation of the biblical message requires a messenger who models what he preaches: "My experience is that is not received as trustworthy if one only talks about things one has not experienced personally. So to lead by telling about things that I experienced a year ago or yesterday [makes it more influential]."

Second, modeling is not limited to certain aspects of the leader's ministry or doing, but includes his entire life and being. P1 described how it was impossible for him to reduce the ministry to merely one aspect of his life. He is a pastor all the time; it is a lifestyle, not primarily a job. It follows that leadership through modeling involves every facet of his life:

> I want people to see my life . . . and see that I live in a way that is credible and trustworthy. The way I manage my time, treat my children, spend my money, and that sort of things. Yes, I try to be a role model in the way I live, with lots of self-irony and humor because I do not always live up to the standard.

P2 admits that the responsibility that comes with leadership in the Pentecostal congregation is burdensome, especially the question of how the church is impacted by his personal and spiritual life:

> And then I start to worry, "is my life and example determinate for the growth of our church?" I have thought a lot about this, . . . the stewardship of my life. Are there any visible results from my use of money that contributes positively or negatively in the congregation? My prayer life, my faith, my failures, my weaknesses?

In summary, P4's description of holistic leadership represents the experience of leadership among the participants:

> I feel that I lead all the time . . . And I believe that in an integrated job as a Christian leader, no one takes a pause [because] what you say and do is important for the message you send. I am the message. In social media, in conversations, in the text message one night to the worship leader who nearly fainted after [several] services. I lead in all these situations.

This brings the argument full circle back to the first constituent—that is, the leader's commitment to a higher purpose as a prime motivation in his ministry and life. Put differently, Pentecostal leadership flows out of being and cannot be addressed without including the leader's entire orientation to life. The leader and his leadership is inextricably connected.

Chapter Summary

This chapter reports the results of the descriptive phenomenological analysis of Pentecostal leadership based on the experiences of Norwegian pastors. Enhanced by the procedure of free imaginative variation, the method was used to identify a general structure of Pentecostal leadership that goes beyond individual and empirical experiences to describe the essence of the phenomenon. This structure, together with its integrated constituents, represents an original contribution to our understanding of Pentecostal leadership. As stated at the outset of the chapter, the constituents are not separate elements, but interrelated and interdependent dimensions of the phenomenon that together make the gestalt of leadership in Pentecostalism. Now that the results have been detected and articulated within the phenomenological attitude, it is time to open the brackets and allow the findings to shed light on existing theories and interpretations and vice versa. This is addressed next.

6

New Findings in Dialogue with Present Understandings

As STATED IN THE introductory chapter, the overall research agenda of this book is to address the question of the meaning of Pentecostal leadership with the purpose of describing its essential features. To reach this goal, relevant literature was reviewed, and the phenomenological analysis of lived experiences performed, culminating in the general structure and the explication of empirical variations presented in the previous chapter. The purpose of this and the next chapter, then, is to show what these new insights mean for the understanding of Pentecostal leadership and to discuss the new findings within the larger field of religious and organizational leadership studies. It is impossible to grasp Pentecostal leadership within a singular theoretical frame, and the discussion, therefore, draws on insights from theology, sociology, and psychology, in addition to organizational leadership research. Since the findings are based on a phenomenological analysis that goes beyond the empirical material, the chapter only sparsely refers to interview data. To base the argument directly on the participants' statements would mean a return to descriptions given in the natural attitude and, consequently, an undermining of the entire purpose of the phenomenological analysis.

In terms of organization, the discussion is ordered around the eight constituents that support the structure. Some constituents are theoretically riper and more complex than others, and no attempts were made to keep the sections at equal length. Given the interdependency between constituents, discussions on each could not be isolated, and some issues are, therefore, treated several times or discussed under one heading when they also could have belonged elsewhere. As with the explication of the constituents in chapter 5, meaning should be sought in the sum of the discussion, not in the separate parts. The overall results are then discussed vis-à-vis extant leadership theories and research before an integrative dialogue, including implications, limitations, and suggestions for further research, concludes the study.

Discussion on Constituents

Motivated by a Sense of Higher, Divine Purpose

The review of the literature in chapter 3 showed that Pentecostal leaders base their leadership on a deep sense of God's calling. In contrast, current findings suggested that this is not always the case. The participants do not univocally affirm the critical role of calling in Pentecostal leadership identity, and the study thus expands the understanding of what causes people to enter pastoral ministry in Pentecostalism by proposing that motivation is better understood in terms of commitment to God's purpose than as calling to a specific ministry. Such motivation may, of course, include a personal sense of calling, but does not rely on it.

Having said that, one is tempted to speculate whether the differences among the participants reflect variance in wording rather than meaning. Eskilt's research on understandings of the missionary call in the Mission Covenant Church of Norway revealed that there has been a change in the perception of calling from the missionary veterans of the pre-WWII generation to the Generation X missionaries born in the 1970s.[1] Eskilt detected a "subjective turn" among missionaries in the generation of 1968 and onwards, implying a shift in commitment from external authorities to obligation to one's authentic self. This shift has ramifications for experiences of calling:

> The understanding of the call as a watershed, life-changing experience has to a great extent been replaced by a greater emphasis on calling as a process. This likely applies to the call to salvation as well as to ministry. At the same time, the "mystical" call endures in a parallel existence with other ways to perceive calling.[2]

1. Eskilt, "Misjonærkallet."
2. Eskilt, "Misjonærkallet," 16. Translation.

If calling is understood processually rather than punctually, as an inner confirmation of God-given gifts and potential rather than an external duty, the differences between the participants are probably smaller than one might assume from a surface reading of their descriptions.

Eskilt's observation of a subjective turn in the understanding of missionary calling parallels the heightened awareness of spiritual matters in contemporary Western culture, a development that spills over on organizational research. As shown in chapter 1, calling language has found its way into the mainstream leadership discourse with the increased interest in organizational spirituality over the last decades. Most observers have agreed that calling is something deeply personal, yet they differ in what constitutes its core[3] and whether this sense of meaning and purpose in work stems from external summons or results from internal self-reflection.[4] In regard to the latter, the results from the present inquiry clearly point to a cause external to the individual as a source for leadership motivation.

Specifically, the incentive to lead stems not only from something beyond the leader, but from someone. The participants' motivation is clearly theocentric, involving a relationship with and reliance upon God in the outworking of their ministry. In this way, it exceeds—though not necessarily supplants—the emphasis on intrinsic motivation and personal authenticity in value-based leadership theories. Servant leadership, in particular, draws attention to leadership motivation, epitomized in Greenleaf's famous dictum: "The Servant leader is servant first. . . . It begins with the natural feeling that one wants to serve, to serve first."[5] Given this emphasis on motivation, Dierendonck finds it surprising how little attention motivational aspects of servant leadership have received.[6] Only recently has the motivational and psychological rationale to engage in servant leadership begun to be explicitly identified.[7] From a theological vantage point, critics have pointed out that Greenleaf's natural feeling to serve is not necessarily natural at all.[8] In a study of servant leadership in the Fourth Gospel, Åkerlund concludes,

---

3. Bunderson and Thompson, "Call of the Wild."

4. Hirschi, "Callings in Career."

5. Greenleaf, *Servant Leadership*, 27.

6. Dierendonck, "Servant Leadership," 1244.

7. Sun, "Servant Identity."

8. Åkerlund, "Son, Sent, and Servant," 8–9.

> Whereas Greenleaf finds the calling to serve in the longing of the human spirit, the Johannine account clearly ties Jesus' service to the divine initiative. . . . The motivation to serve does not evolve out of thin air but rather comes from a sense of being called and commissioned to serve—not only something but—someone beyond oneself.[9]

This study seems to support the claim by showing how the participants are propelled into leadership, not primarily by some natural inclination, but through their relationship with God and an understanding of his purpose.

This finding corresponds with Miller and Yamamori, who highlight the critical role of a divine-human encounter in empowering and enabling people to be servants of others. They conclude, "While organizational structure is an important ingredient, the driving force behind the social ministries of Pentecostals is their experience of the Spirit in moments of worship."[10] This project suggests a similar dynamic: Pentecostal leadership flows out of a higher sense of purpose derived from a life-changing encounter with God—abruptly through a specific calling experience, or gradually through an emerging sense of destiny to serve God's mission as an ecclesial leader. The goal here is not to pit this theocentric understanding of leadership motivation up against Greenleaf's natural feeling to serve, but to show how leadership in this ecclesial setting (and probably others) takes its cues and impetus from an agent apart from the leader himself. This is a distinct element that must be accounted for in describing the phenomenon, and one that might easily be overlooked when leadership in the ecclesial organization is neatly conceptualized along the lines of organizational leadership theories. Pentecostal leadership, it seems, begins with God's initiative and continues with a sense of leading in his name and on his behalf. Attempts to describe the phenomenon that do not take this constituent into consideration run the risk of ignoring one of its essential characteristics.

Derived Leadership

As seen in the previous chapter, relations with the divine not only motivate the participants to take on leadership roles in Pentecostal congregations, but continue as an ongoing sense of leading on behalf of God in their ministerial responsibilities. This understanding of leadership is embedded in a

9. Åkerlund, "Son, Sent, and Servant," 8–9.

10. Miller and Yamamori, *Global Pentecostalism*, 221.

distinct Pentecostal theology proper. Pentecostals' relationships with and expectations of God are "based on a belief that he is vibrant, active and able to wisely set the agenda for his world."[11] As such, Pentecostals have a distinct understanding of the relationality of God, a theology in which God is interactive and willingly invites believers to participate with him in working out his will in real partnership.[12] Tangen notes,

> From a theological perspective, spiritual leadership in the sense of centering or integrating everything around God can be considered the primary and ultimate goal of all leadership. . . . God is also the primary source of authority, and the first task of leadership is therefore to relate to him through the means of grace in the Spirit. Charisma then is primarily a relation, and only secondarily a "possession" of gifts.[13]

Albrecht and Howard suggest that Pentecostal spirituality "is hardwired to perceive and respond to the influences of the Holy Spirit."[14] The predisposition to expect that God will act and the accompanied attention to the Spirit's leading are expressions of this sentiment. It follows that it is essential for the Pentecostal leader to discern what God says and does, as is evident in the participants' emphasis on constantly turning one's attention to God in their leadership. God is active and, therefore, the Pentecostal leader must be the same way: "God has 'broken in' to this world through the Spirit of Christ, invading it with an existentially real and tangible encounter with the Lord Jesus Christ himself."[15]

This view not only says something about how Pentecostals perceive God, but also about how they view the world. Observers within and outside the movement have pointed out that the Pentecostal ethos is something more than evangelicalism plus tongues; it represents a worldview with an experiential epistemology.[16] While the centrality of experience will be discussed in the section on Pentecostal tradition, it must be said that the Pentecostal worldview represents what Poloma and Green describe as a "curious blend of premodern miracles, modern technology, and postmod-

11. Warrington, *Pentecostal Theology*, 29.

12. Warrington, *Pentecostal Theology*, 33.

13. Tangen, *Ecclesial Identification*, 334.

14. Albrecht and Howard, "Pentecostal Spirituality," 240.

15. Albrecht and Howard, "Pentecostal Spirituality," 244.

16. See Johns, "Yielding to the Spirit"; Poloma and Green, *Assemblies of God*; Smith, *Thinking in Tongues*; Warrington, *Pentecostal Theology*, 20–27.

ern mysticism in which the natural blends with the supernatural."[17] This inclusion of the supernatural in Pentecostal cosmology to a great extent explains its growth in the Global South[18] and flows out of a distinct Pentecostal *Weltanschauung.*

According to Smith, this worldview consists of (a) a radical openness to God and the notion that he may do something new or different, (b) an enchanted theology of culture and creation, (c) a non-dualistic affirmation of materiality, (d) a narrative-affective epistemology, and (e) an eschatological orientation to mission and justice.[19] In particular, the second and third points are relevant for the present discussion, as they highlight the ongoing activity of God in the individual and the world. The experience of the fullness of the Spirit is the crux of Pentecostal theology, and this is embedded in a holistic worldview where the Spirit is involved in every aspect of individual and communal life.[20] As shown by Land, Pentecostals hold that God has not only acted generally in history, but specifically in their history.[21] The ongoing action of God is, therefore, crucial and decisive, and "to live in the presence of the God of redemption is to live as a participant in the divine drama."[22] In Smith's terms, Pentecostals see the world as enchanted because of the Spirit's presence and immanence within the created order.[23]

Since the Spirit is active in the world, it is a prime responsibility for the Pentecostal leader to determine where God is at work and join in. Discernment is a key word here. Albrecht and Howard argue that attention to the Spirit is central to Pentecostal spirituality as "a kind of radical receptivity to this activity of the Spirit, a softness to changes in intuition and feeling that indicate the direction of the winds of the Spirit."[24] As demonstrated in chapter 5, the participants to various degrees express this sentiment in their accounts of habitually turning to God in prayer, protecting and promoting a sensitivity to the Spirit's urgings, and receiving specific revelation about

17. Poloma and Green, *Assemblies of God*, loc. 1316.

18. Anderson, *Introduction to Pentecostalism*, 195–205; Yung, "Integrity of Mission."

19. Smith, *Thinking in Tongues.*

20. Anderson, *Introduction to Pentecostalism*, 196–97.

21. Land, *Pentecostal Spirituality*, 135.

22. Land, *Pentecostal Spirituality*, 197.

23. Smith, *Thinking in Tongues*, loc. 880–903. Pentecostal cosmology describes a world inhabited not only by the Holy Spirit, but also evil spirits. While Pentecostals in the West are somewhat neutralized to this premodern worldview, it is reflected in the practices of spiritual warfare in (neo-)Pentecostal groups, predominantly in the Global South.

24. Albrecht and Howard, "Pentecostal Spirituality," 241.

what they should do. Also, to various extents, the participants rely on spiritual gifts in making decisions. The belief in this capacity to discern God's will through the practice of charismatic gifts is a unique contribution of the Pentecostal movement, and echoes the Pentecostal emphasis on experience in discerning where God is at work. In Kim's words, "If the Holy Spirit is understood as a person with whom it is possible to have relationship, it is reasonable to suppose that it involves emotion and intuition, as well as intelligence."[25]

Parker confirms this point, but warns against seeing Pentecostal discernment as a unidimensional exercise where charismatic manifestations are the sole means of determination.[26] In a comprehensive study on Pentecostal discernment and decision-making, he shows that Pentecostals, like other groups, make decisions in various ways, and not always with reference to the Spirit. The empirical findings in the present project confirm this conclusion and show that Pentecostal leaders employ several strategies when they seek to discern God's will and lead on his behalf.

While Parker focuses primarily on situations where the leading of the Spirit is experienced as an extraordinary presence, he confirms some of the broader tendencies observed in the present work. First, he highlights the communal character of discernment and decision-making, a point evident in the participants' descriptions and shared by others who have proposed models of decision-making in Pentecostal-charismatic organizations.[27] Second, he sanctions a point alluded above and shared among most of the participants, namely that leadership decisions in Pentecostalism not only stem from cognitive rationality, but also incorporate the whole person in leading.

> "Feelings" connected to issues under consideration are understood, not as "things that get in the way" of decision making[sic], but as important and necessary to good decision making[sic]. In Pentecostal terms, this element is a recognition that the Spirit transcends the strictly rational process of decision making[sic] to work at the affective, intuitive level as well.[28]

This does not, of course, imply that the Spirit is absent in rational processes, or that Pentecostal decision-making refrains from using functional rationality. On the contrary, Parker underlines the need for holistic knowing, in

---

25. Kim, *Holy Spirit in the World*, 169.

26. Parker, *Led by the Spirit*.

27. Johns, "Formational Leadership."

28. Parker, *Led by the Spirit*, 212.

which reason and Spirit are not pitted against each other. As mentioned by the participants and discussed in the literature,[29] when discernment proceeds to decision-making, it may incorporate insights from the humanities and organizational leadership, in addition to the intuitive and spiritual aspects of discernment discussed here. This integrative approach to leadership illustrates how Pentecostal leaders may draw from several faculties in leading the congregation, a point to be discussed next.

Human and Divine Agency in a Seamless Interaction Between Rationality and Spirituality

As described in chapter 5, the phenomenological analysis indicates that the sense of being led by a God who is active in every aspect of life frees the Pentecostal leader to proactively engage in organizational matters and seamlessly combine spirituality and rationality in doing so. This finding matches Wacker's claim that Pentecostal cosmology downplays the separation between the visible and the invisible, worships a "God with skin,"[30] and boldly engages in the present affairs based on their distinct understanding of how God wants to do something here and now: "The otherworldly legitimates the thisworldy."[31] Lindhardt's study of Chilean Pentecostalism shows a similar dynamic.[32] Albeit powerless and marginalized in any conventional meaning of what it means to have influence, Lindhardt observes that Pentecostal believers, "by accepting and even idealizing human powerlessness and total dependence upon God, in fact nurture a certain sense of agency and power."[33] Put differently, their understanding of divine intervention and agency shape their interpretation of everyday events, and allows for the cultivation of a certain sense of power and agency. While they trust in the sovereignty of God even to the point of fatalism, they also believe that human agents are important in the outworking of the sacred will—evident in their emphasis on prayer, evangelism, Bible reading, and ritual practice. As such, they indirectly feel a responsibility to act upon the social world through power and agency within a theistic religious frame.[34]

29. See Kaak, Lemaster, and Muthiah, "Integrative Decision-Making."

30. Wacker, *Heaven Below*, 87.

31. Wacker, *Heaven Below*, 268.

32. Lindhardt, *Power in Powerlessness*.

33. Lindhardt, *Power in Powerlessness*, 10.

34. See also Smilde, "Letting God Govern," 290.

In a similar vein, Johns notes how the experientially God-centered worldview of Pentecostalism predisposes the Spirit-filled believer to see "God at work in, with, through, above, and beyond all events. Therefore, all space is sacred space and all time is sacred time."[35] Consequently, Pentecostal leaders may expect that God may manifest himself in new and innovative ways with no historical precedence,[36] as witnessed by the participants' disposition to lead the organization in novel ways and into unexploited domains. This finding corresponds with a larger shift within the Norwegian Pentecostal movement, described by Maurset as a transition from a holiness movement to a market movement with more open attitudes toward the wider culture.[37] From a global perspective, Miller and Yamamori observe that newer strands of Pentecostalism tend to downplay the focus on personal purity among older generations of sectarian Pentecostals in favor of a more active engagement in worldly affairs:

> Progressive Pentecostals do not separate Christians from the world of everyday trade and commerce in an artificial attempt to maintain their holiness. Instead, they seek to model their behavior after the lifestyle of Jesus, who constantly blurred the line between the sacred and profane worlds, mixing with sinners and those in need as much, or more, than he did with religious leaders and those concerned about their external righteousness.[38]

The present project and Maurset's analysis indicate a similar trend in Norwegian Pentecostalism. The reference to blurring lines between the sacred and profane in the literature and among the participants is important here. Pentecostal spirituality represents an understanding of the world that overcomes any sacred/secular divides[39] and enables the leader to draw on functional rationality in spiritual matters and vice versa.[40] Arguably, these beliefs together generate confidence to act innovatively and go beyond conventional rationality to dare and endure things that would otherwise seem impossible. If God is at work everywhere, the Pentecostal leader may seamlessly combine spiritual disciplines, human reasoning, and pragmatic consideration in working out what he perceives to be God's purposes for

35. Johns, "Yielding to the Spirit," 75.
36. Warrington, *Pentecostal Theology*, 24–25.
37. Maurset, "Frå Helgingsrørsle til Marknadsrørsle."
38. Miller and Yamamori, *Global Pentecostalism*, 59.
39. Smith, *Thinking in Tongues*, 24.
40. Parker, *Led by the Spirit*, 114.

the organization. Again, this stems from a worldview that downplays the distinction between spiritual and practical and maintains that the leader may hear from God as part of his leadership in both realms. The God who is active in the world does not stop at the door to the church, but is also active in culture and creation. Research that strongly contrasts the spiritual and the material therefore misses a central tenet of Pentecostalism.[41] The Pentecostal imagination sees both realms as God-infused, and the Pentecostal leader is hence free to draw on spiritual and cognitive capacities simultaneously. While this interaction between spirituality and rationality may be seamless, the following constituent demonstrates that it is not conflictless.

Pragmatic and Eclectic Stance Toward the Pentecostal Tradition

As discussed in chapter 2, the quest for an essential Pentecostal identity has shown itself to be notoriously difficult due to the vast variety within the movement(s). This is something to be observed rather than solved. What is of interest here is how leaders see it as a part of their leadership to define for the congregation what Pentecostal spirituality should look like in time and space—"[it] is highly subjective, therefore we must take a subjective responsibility to define our spirituality" (P3). A debate in *Korsets Seier*, the weekly newspaper of the Norwegian Pentecostal movement, illustrates the point. In defense of restricting charismatic utterances in public gatherings, a younger church planter stated,

> That speaking in tongues no longer characterizes Pentecostal worship services is not a sign of apostasy. The attention is turned from speaking in tongues to [speaking] a language that makes the Gospel understandable. But we don't stop speaking in tongues. We must create arenas both in the family and the congregation where speaking in tongues and prayer is natural.[42]

The following week, a reader accused Pentecostal leaders of being both afraid and embarrassed in downplaying tongues, and asked Kvammen rhetorically, "When did you get permission from the Holy Spirit to move him here or there?"[43] It is not surprising that discussions like this gain much

41. Meyer, "Aesthetics of Persuasion," 751–53.

42. Kvammen, "Tungetalen Flyttes," 14.

43. Kesseboom, "Pinseleiarene Er Redde og Flaue," 33.

steam in the Pentecostal movement since "spirituality [in Pentecostalism] is frequently defined within the context of a church service more than a devotional closet."[44] Pentecostal spirituality is certainly more than speaking in tongues, but the accentuation of this particular charism in the movement makes it a good showcase for how leaders influence the congregation by framing its spirituality and drawing selectively from its history.

Observers of Pentecostalism in Norway[45] and in the United States[46] note a privatization of tongues and a parallel decline of speaking in tongues in public gatherings. Maurset speculates that this tendency partly stems from an increased emphasis on leadership in the Norwegian Pentecostal movement. In any case, this development is interesting in relation to studies of Pentecostal leadership because the removal of tongues excludes a democratic element from the Pentecostal congregation. The privatization of glossolalia arguably entails a change in symmetry between leaders and congregation and is consequently more than a practical regulation of spirituality. As has been mentioned above, the open access to the charismatic Spirit is a strong egalitarian impulse in Pentecostalism.

According to Albrecht and Howard, the emphasis on the charismata obliges Pentecostals to encourage participation in the church based on the gifts the Spirit has bestowed on each member.[47] They should thus understand themselves as a fluid and coparticipating organization in which "leadership in a congregation may arise at any moment as any sister or brother becomes the vehicle for the authoritative word or touch of God in the midst of the gathering."[48] Lie suggests that the pouring out of the Spirit "on all people" (Joel 2:28) implies a democratization of the Spirit where differences between leaders and congregation are downplayed.[49] The gifts of tongues and interpretation, in particular, give the common church member the right to participate—even interfere—in the service on equal footing with the preacher. As reported by two eyewitnesses,

> The preacher is stopped in the middle of a sentence . . . The one interrupting is an ordinary member of the congregation. The janitor at the local public school or one of the workers at the mill . . .

44. McMahan, "Spiritual Direction," 152–53.

45. Maurset, "Frå Helgingsrørsle til Marknadsrørsle."

46. Poloma and Green, *Assemblies of God.*

47. Albrecht and Howard, "Pentecostal Spirituality."

48. Albrecht and Howard, "Pentecostal Spirituality," 243.

49. Lie, "Fra Pinsevenn."

> The prophetic message can come to each and every one. God's
> gifts are given to all, *independent* of personal status. The form of
> worship service in the Pentecostal movement is among the most
> anti-authoritarian and egalitarian in Norwegian church life.[50]

Lie fears that the current emphasis on pastoral and organizational leadership in the Norwegian and global Pentecostal movement terminates this
democratic bent. Once someone understands oneself as leader and others
as followers, Lie contends that genuine church life and normal interper-
sonal relationships are demolished.

I think that Lie overestimates both the egalitarianism of early Pentecostalism and the negative consequences of leadership-thinking in the contemporary movement. That everyone can partake spontaneously in church
meetings does not necessarily equal equality; it might just as well regress
into informal and dysfunctional leadership structures where some strong
individuals subdue others in the name of the Lord. Neither do limitations
in the use of tongues in public gatherings mean that Pentecostal leadership
automatically becomes more hierarchical. Interestingly, the leader who is
most hostile toward free-floating charisma among the participants (P1) is
also the one who speaks most vividly about decision-making in teams.

Regulations of charismatic utterings in Pentecostal churches cannot be
settled here and are somewhat secondary to the thrust of this study. What is
highly relevant, however, is that leaders do not merely change methods but
profoundly shape Pentecostal identity. The relationship between content
and container is very complex, and one inevitably alters the former when
one changes the latter. In encouraging some spiritual practices and discour-
aging others, Pentecostal leaders take the role of gatekeepers who define the
space within which spirituality may operate. To give it a negative slant, the
Spirit blows wherever it wills—as long as it is within the boundaries established by the leader. This is an overly cynical conclusion, however. Albrecht
shows that, although the congregation participates in Pentecostal meetings and thereby moves toward egalitarian forms of liturgical leadership,
there are distinct leadership identities.[51] According to Albrecht, appointed
leaders function as (a) facilitators/coordinators of the liturgy, (b) experts
in specialized areas such as teaching and preaching, and (c) authorities in
sanctioning the charismatic expression. He states, "While each ritualist
evaluates, discerns and analyzes, most look for a signal from an established

---

50. Dahl and Rudolph, *Fra Seier til Nederlag*, 99–100. Translation. Emphasis original.

51. Albrecht, *Rites in the Spirit*.

liturgical leader (e.g., a pastor) to authenticate the charismatic utterance or performance."[52] The pastor inhabits this role, as the gift to do so has been recognized in him. The more this gift is recognized by the community, the more authority the leader has in liturgy and beyond as reflected in P4's stress on leading by "the speed of trust" since leaders do not have more leadership than the trust they have earned.

The eclectic position toward the Pentecostal heritage is not without risks. When treating the tradition as a resource rather than a source, the Pentecostal leader runs the risk of missing some of the movement's basic characteristics. Several of Pentecostalism's authoritative students hold that the early and formative years of Pentecostalism represent the heart, rather than the infancy, of the movement's spirituality.[53] Further, transforming experiences with God are at the heart of a distinct Pentecostal worldview, making the filling of the Spirit a normative epistemological framework that changes the structures through which the individual understands the world.[54] With this backdrop, Poloma and Green fear that "the essence of Pentecostalism as a 'new paradigm'—with the natural and supernatural engaged in a dialectic dance—is compromised by accommodative forces that threaten to dilute Pentecostal identity."[55] In a similar vein, McGee suspects, "The supernatural worldview that has undergirded Pentecostalism and differentiated it most from Evangelicalism now stands in jeopardy."[56] Assumingly, the Pentecostal movement is in a state of identity crisis.

Yet this wrestle for identity is not new, but has followed the movement since its outset early in the twentieth century.[57] In Pentecostalism, diversity has always been a given:

> Like most religious groups comprised of diverse elements, the Pentecostal movement has a mixed identity, rife with the potential for creating polarizing tendencies within its various constituents and for generating psychological splitting within its individual participants.[58]

---

52. Albrecht, *Rites in the Spirit*, 140.

53. E.g., Hollenweger, *Pentecostals*; Land, *Pentecostal Spirituality*, 14–15, 47.

54. Johns, "Yielding to the Spirit," 74–76.

55. Poloma and Green, *Assemblies of God*, loc. 1275.

56. McGee, "More than Evangelical," 299.

57. Dempster, "Search for Pentecostal Identity," 1–2; Jacobsen, *Thinking in the Spirit*, 10–12.

58. Dempster, "Search for Pentecostal Identity," 5.

Thus, the question is not if the movement handles diversity, but how to do it, and what role ecclesial leaders play in this identity work. When new generations of Pentecostal leaders seek to define spirituality in and for their congregation, as do the participants in this study, they are, in certain aspects, in continuity with earlier leaders in the movement—albeit their understanding and praxis of Pentecostal spirituality may look different from that of their forerunners. When P1 asks, "What is God doing in our time? What does the Spirit say to the churches? They [previous leaders] saw themselves merely as defenders [of the tradition]," he echoes first-generation Pentecostal leaders who were more interested in what God was actually doing in the world than what the theological tradition claimed God was supposed to be doing.[59] When P3 suggests that leaders must define the spirituality of the Pentecostal congregation, he affirms that Pentecostalism by its very nature is a work in progress that cannot be brought to a well-ordered closure.[60]

On the contrary, "Pentecostal theology at its best is not spoon-fed to people or crammed down their throats but is constantly being rearticulated at the local level in ways that ring true to people's life experiences and the experiences of their communities."[61] Thus, to be a Pentecostal leader is closer to attending a jazz-jam than joining a symphonic orchestra. There is room for improvisation with a band of others who play to the same tune. Yet, there is a groove, a rhythm, some melody lines that all must adhere to; not everything will go. In a similar vein, the Pentecostal leader is "linked to communities of discernment (denominations, congregations, small groups, and families) that act as hedges on unfettered spiritual creativity."[62] The community is a bearer of the tradition, and leaders must thus be sensitive to the community in defining and articulating the direction and spirituality of the congregation.[63] This underlines the reciprocal character of Pentecostal leadership discussed in the section about the dialectic relationship between structure and agency.

The critical reflection on tradition among the participants is perhaps primarily a signal of a maturing Pentecostalism. One must not forget that early Pentecostal leaders—fueled by strong mission commitment and eschatological urgency—often promoted a pragmatism that developed into unreflective

59. Jacobsen, *Thinking in the Spirit*, 360.
60. Jacobsen, *Thinking in the Spirit*, 353.
61. Jacobsen, *Thinking in the Spirit*, 363.
62. Jacobsen, *Thinking in the Spirit*, 363.
63. Chan, *Pentecostal Theology*, 17–18.

activism and anti-intellectualism.[64] The challenge for Pentecostal leaders, then, is to hold in fruitful tension their confessional tradition—Christian and Pentecostal—and the need for cultural relevance. This can hardly take place without thorough reflection on both. Kärkkäinen asserts,

> Pentecostals have been very slow to acknowledge the meaning of culture to proclamation. In their own distinctive—one could perhaps say, unthematized way—Pentecostals have reacted to culture by devising all kinds of contextual methods of evangelization and church planting. . . . But this has not been a result of a sustained reflection but rather an outcome of a highly practical mission strategy.[65]

If the Pentecostal movement is in a period of theological adolescence, as Johns and Land claim,[66] Pentecostals are asked to choose who they will be, to revision their present and future identity in light of their past. Such work requires gifted and careful leadership and a respectful yet realistic look upon their spiritual mothers and fathers.[67] In Chan's words, "critical self-reflection is essential when a movement matures."[68] In order to grow up, not only grow older, Johns suggests that the Pentecostal movement may choose between growth by substation and growth by integration.[69] The former describes a patchwork identity comprised of thoughts, beliefs, affections, and actions copied from others. Since there is no inner consistent core, groups with such identities will continually struggle with who they are. Growth by integration, on the other hand, is the more time-consuming path because it requires attention to familial background stories and the integration of these in one's own narrative. It is a more stable identity, but one that involves self-reflection and calls for differentiation, an understanding of how one is like—and different from—others. Johns admits that it would be easy for Pentecostals to grow by substitution; after all, "they have partners and a larger consumer culture ready to provide the pieces with which to construct an identity."[70] To do so, however, would be to give up on the notion that there is such a thing as "a 'Pentecostal identity,' a core of who they

64. McGee, "More than Evangelical," 299.
65. Kärkkäinen, "'Culture, Contextualization, and Conversion,'" 274.
66. Land, Pentecostal Spirituality; Johns, "Adolescence of Pentecostalism."
67. Land, Pentecostal Spirituality, 190–91.
68. Chan, Pentecostal Theology, 20.
69. Johns, "Adolescence of Pentecostalism."
70. Johns, "Adolescence of Pentecostalism," 11.

are which may be different from and yet alike others."[71] In contrast to this approach, Johns pleads that Pentecostals choose maturity through growth by integration and embrace a distinct and courageous self-understanding. This includes a qualified, second naiveté recovery of the initial impulses of the movement with its own mission and agenda.[72]

The results of the current study indicate that Johns' plea is answered, at least partly. The participants reflect on and draw from the Pentecostal tradition as part of their leadership, even though there are differences between them in terms of how binding they understood the tradition to be. The point here is not to define Pentecostal orthodoxy, but to highlight the wide-ranging consequences leadership decisions have on aspects of ecclesial life beyond those typically associated with organizational leadership. The study emphasizes the role of ecclesial leadership in defining "whither Pentecostalism"[73] should prevail. The picking and choosing from the menu of Pentecostal spirituality is social influence—leadership indeed and in deed—but one that happens more subtly than proclamation of grand dreams and visions. Also, the argument underlines the intricate and intrinsic interplay between spiritual and practical matters in Pentecostal leadership discussed in the previous section.

I concluded in chapter 5 that the eclectic and pragmatic stance toward the Pentecostal tradition is a two-edged sword. On one side, the freedom from binding traditions may degenerate into uncritical utilitarian emphasis on visible success and numerical growth. Commenting on neo-Pentecostal networks in the United Kingdom, Kay observes,

> There are indications that, in some places, business practices supersede theological practices. Indeed, where Christian churches talk about their "brand" rather than their theology, it is time to ask serious questions about how long such groupings will last. Theology within the networks . . . functions as motivational and value-laden discourse and loses its traditional normative role; remove normativity and there is nothing beyond pragmatics by which the church guides itself. The concept of the church as the people of God in the presence of God is lost and, instead of a community inspired by the Holy Spirit, we see an agency designed to hit certain

71. Johns, "Adolescence of Pentecostalism," 11.

72. Faupel, "Whither Pentecostalism."

73. Faupel, "Whither Pentecostalism."

targets using inflexible procedures drawn from the worlds of business and management.[74]

The methodology utilized in the present project does not explore whether the same development takes place in Norwegian Pentecostalism because it addresses the meaning Pentecostal leaders make of their leadership rather than the results thereof. Still, the participants' reflection about the risk of an overly practical approach to church ministry indicates that the problem at least surfaces on their radar.

On the other side, the fluid relationship to traditions provides freedom and flexibility for innovation and adaptability. Albrecht and Howard observe that "Pentecostals have a certain knack for improvisation"[75] that make them effective and able to adapt to new situations and contexts. As shown from the review of the extant literature, Pentecostals have been keen to contextualize their message and forms of leadership. This was also a hallmark of early Pentecostalism, as evident in Wacker's analysis of the movement and his emphasis on the interaction between primitivism and pragmatism throughout its history.[76] It is likely that this down-to-earth, this-worldly approach to Christianity partly explains why Pentecostalism is so attractive to many people.[77] Pentecostals have always had a leaning toward the empirical—toward works in practice—yet within the boundaries of biblical authority.[78] In this regard, the Pentecostal leadership described in this study follows in the footsteps of their spiritual ancestors.

Persuasive Communication

The literature review showed that recounts of calling narratives function as legitimizing devices for the leaders in Pentecostal groups.[79] This aspect of narrative leadership did not surface as essential in the descriptions of Pentecostal leadership detected in this study. Yet, persuasive communication remains central to Pentecostal leadership on a phenomenological level. To begin with, persuasive communication is central to all leadership,

74. Kay, "Apostolic Networks in Britain," 22.

75. Albrecht and Howard, "Pentecostal Spirituality," 243.

76. Wacker, *Heaven Below*.

77. Cox, "Personal Reflection," 31.

78. Holm, "Varieties of Pentecostal Experience"; Neumann, *Pentecostal Experience*, 151–58.

79. Währisch-Oblau, *Missionary Self-Perception*, 86.

as interaction through language is embedded in the very phenomenon of leadership as a social process. At its core, "leadership is human (symbolic) communication,"[80] and the ability to inspire others through motivational communication, therefore, may be described as "the language of leadership."[81] In the same token, Gardner argues that leaders achieve their effectiveness primarily through the communication and performance of narratives that offer meaning and identity to followers.[82] This function of narratives is central to ecclesial leadership, and Hopewell shows how the structuring of symbolic elements into a congregational culture is important in the development and maintenance of group identity:

> Even a plain church on a pale day catches one in a deep current of narrative interpretation and representation by which people give sense and order to their lives. Most of this creative stream is unconscious and involuntary, drawing in part upon images lodged long ago in the human struggle for meaning. Thus a congregation is held together by much more than creeds, governing structures, and programs. At a deeper level, it is implicated in the symbols and signals of the world, gathering and grounding them in the congregation's own idiom.[83]

Advocates of constructivist research paradigms have long claimed that organizing and leadership involves the interplay and conflict between networks of communication and meaning,[84] and that organizations are stories in which leaders are intertwined in complex story networks.[85] This narrative turn in leadership and organizational studies[86] parallels a rising awareness of the crucial role narratives play in Pentecostal identity.

According to Smith, Pentecostal epistemology is fundamentally narrative as stories and testimonies take on existential significance as means of identity building.[87] Pentecostalism's oral roots and inclination toward narrative theologizing and sense-making thus make narrative leadership especially potent in Pentecostal circles, as I have demonstrated in a pre-

---

80. Hackman and Johnson, *Leadership*, 12.

81. Conger, "Inspiring Others."

82. Gardner, *Leading Minds*.

83. Hopewell, *Congregation*, 5.

84. Ford, "Organizational Change."

85. Auvinen, "Ghost Leader," 5; Boje et al., "Language and Organization."

86. Czarniawska, *Narratives in Social Science Research*.

87. Smith, *Thinking in Tongues*.

vious work on Thomas Ball Barratt's leadership in the early days of the Norwegian Pentecostal movement.[88]

I suggest that Barratt's leadership did not rest solely on his personal attributes, but on his ability to articulate and interpret his experiences in terms that made sense to his audience. The Pentecostal revival in Norway spread internationally through reports in the international press, through traveling and preaching in various countries, and through the publication of Pentecostal literature in many languages. In all of this, Barratt exercised indirect leadership on a great number of people based on the reports, accounts, and interpretations he gave of the revival he himself took part in. Bundy asserts, "Barratt's influence was established as much by the story of his life, frequently retold, as by the essays and books produced in decades of industrious writings."[89] Bundy even suggests that the narratives recorded in *Byposten*, a weekly newspaper founded by Barratt, initiated revivals throughout Norway and built a network that was central to Barratt's reception in various parts of the country.[90] Thus, I propose that his leadership was irrevocably connected not only to his experience, but also to the narration of it.

This proposal corresponds with Martin's claim that Pentecostal leaders influence more by means of personal stories and imagery than by abstract propositions.[91] This kind of narrative knowledge is more affective than deductive,[92] and its emphasis on experiential spirituality has led some observers to suggest a link between Pentecostalism and postmodernity.[93] While Pentecostalism undeniably tangents some characteristics associated with postmodernity, Kärkkainen notes, "Both Pentecostalisms and postmodernities are formed by and bring about their own particular narratives, [but] behind Pentecostalism there is also a Big Story, the story of the Gospel."[94] Precisely, this reliance on a normative script, evident among the participants' descriptions of their leadership, drives a wedge between Pentecostal spirituality and identity and the relativist tendencies in social constructionism.

88. Åkerlund, "When the Fire Fell," 11–12.

89. Bundy, *Visions of Apostolic Mission*, 133.

90. Bundy, *Visions of Apostolic Mission*, 176–79, 227.

91. Martin, *Pentecostalism*, 167.

92. Smith, *Thinking in Tongues*, 63–65.

93. See discussion in Kärkkäinen, "Re-Turn of Religion."

94. Kärkkäinen, "Re-Turn of Religion," 485.

Because the Pentecostal tradition and spirituality is so loose, unde-fined, and prone to incorporate elements from other traditions and con-text, a wide field of communication opportunities opens for the Pentecostal leader. Narratives are the raw material of leadership, and Pentecostal leaders exercise power in selecting and bending stories in manners that support their agenda. However, their leadership happens within the perim-eter of Scriptural authority. Drawing on Vanhoozer's canonical-linguistic approach to theology,[95] Tangen asserts that "the Christian leader is more than an inspiring motivator, or skilful teacher; he or she must be seen as a dramatic director who helps people to understand and enact the Biblical script, in a specific context."[96] Tangen labels this activity "Theo-dramatic leadership," and maintains that it is grounded in the biblical narrative as it seeks to help congregants see themselves as participating in Theo-drama, the story of God. While the Bible is the normative script for the church, the ecclesial leader is the director who sets the divine drama on stage in the local congregational theatre. In Vanhoozer's words, "The pastor translates and extends canonical practices into congregational practices."[97] As such, the leader is not entirely free to do whatever he pleases. It is the Scripture as script, not his directing, that is normative.

Tangen's research further indicates that preaching and teaching are the most important forms of direct spiritual leadership to enhance follower commitment in the Pentecostal congregations.[98] This finding matches the prominence of preaching in the spiritual development of Pentecostals due to the accentuation of orality and narrative in the movement.[99] In perform-ing the Theo-drama in local congregations, Vanhoozer argues that the sermon—not theories of leadership or management—should be the pas-tor's top priority and prime means of influence in the congregation.[100] The results gleaned from the present study indicate that this is the case among Norwegian Pentecostal leaders. Yet, the participants' stress on preaching as a part of, not aside from, their leadership suggests that Vanhoozer's appar-ent dichotomy between preaching and leadership is a false one.

95. Vanhoozer, *Drama of Doctrine*.

96. Tangen, *Ecclesial Identification*, 329.

97. Vanhoozer, *Drama of Doctrine*, 456.

98. Tangen, *Ecclesial Identification*, 335.

99. Warrington, *Pentecostal Theology*, 201–4.

100. Vanhoozer, *Drama of Doctrine*, 456.

An alternative view is that preaching is a form of leadership in which the preacher leads through the creation of images of an alternative world in the minds of the listeners. By linking Brueggemann's notion of prophetic imagination[101] with contemporary leadership theories, Åkerlund suggests that preaching contributes to Christian leadership when it expresses a coherent story of the biblical witness, an orientation toward the future, and the use of imaginative language.[102] This accentuation of imaginative and symbolic language resembles the growing interest in the role aesthetics play in leadership, generally,[103] and in Pentecostalism, specifically.[104]

In shaping the Pentecostal gathering and drawing the boundaries for desirable expressions, Pentecostal leaders have engaged in what Meyer describes as aesthetics of persuasion.[105] The inclusion of some liturgical elements on the expense of others, as seen in the participants' sifting through the Pentecostal tradition, is thus not merely a question of preference but of power, because religious aesthetics "[authorize] a particular distribution of the sensible that opens up a space for religious experience, yet excludes—or even anesthetizes—other possibilities."[106] P1's statement, "there are thousands of ways to be a church. We choose this," reflects this point.

The role of aesthetics in leadership obviously goes beyond the spoken word, yet verbal communication remains an important aspect of Pentecostal leadership. To quote P1 again, "Through preaching we highlight ideals . . . The sermon [must] be by the Word of God, but it must also be so specific that people know what to do with it. 'How do I live with this?'" In this sense, the participants lead the church through their ability to make sense of current realities and interpret for the congregation both its past and its future. It is not uncommon for Christian leaders to see their role as interpreters of what is going on to the wider community. To do so may be especially important in charismatic circles where the work of the Spirit is not perceived as such by all. Peter's address to the crowd in Acts 2:15–16 illustrates the point: "These people are not drunk, as you suppose . . . No, this

101. Brueggemann, *Prophetic Imagination*; Brueggemann, *Practice of Prophetic Imagination*.

102. Åkerlund, "Preaching as Christian Leadership."

103. Duke, "Aesthetics of Leadership"; Hansen et al., "Aesthetic Leadership."

104. Klaver, "Pentecostal Pastorpreneurs"; Meyer, "Aesthetics of Persuasion," 754–58; Tangen, *Ecclesial Identification*, 187–89.

105. Meyer, "Aesthetics of Persuasion."

106. Meyer, "Aesthetics of Persuasion," 755.

is what was spoken by the prophet Joel." In a similar vein, leaders of charismatic revivals often use testimonial narratives to explain and interpret what was happening as signals of God's presence[107] or to bolster their own leadership.[108] Further, Jacobsen points out that words have creative powers as a means to interpret religious experiences after they occur.[109] Leaders cannot control what people experience, but they can provide meaning to their experiences *ex post facto* by explicating that which elsewhere would remain obscure. This way they promote some experiences and negate others and influence congregational spirituality and identity indirectly through persuasive communication.

A question lingers in the background of the above argument: If the Pentecostal leader influences by interpreting events and making sense of reality on behalf of the congregation, what then if his authority is disputed? An eyewitness to a battle for control in a Pentecostal organization remarked, "Again and again the debate returned to an underlying theological impasse: with whom does the final authority for a God-given vision lie?"[110] This statement epitomizes the complex and unruly leadership dynamics in Pentecostal congregations where the leader's authority oscillates between personal and formal bases. To lead is to set direction for the organization, but the leader's ability to do so is contingent upon the organization's recognition of his leadership. This paradoxical relationship is addressed next.

Dialectic Relationship Between Structure and Agency

Wacker holds that primitive and pragmatic impulses were yoked together in early American Pentecostalism, making it possible to "balance the most eye-popping features of the supernatural with the most chest-thumping features of the natural."[111] Wacker's main thesis is that the genius of the Pentecostal movement lies precisely in its ability to hold these apparently incompatible impulses in creative tension, a tension that parallels what is described as a dialectic relationship between structure and agency in the current study. According to Poloma, this paradox is built into the DNA of Pentecostalism and manifests itself in the pull between charisma and

107. Cartledge, *Testimony in the Spirit*, 92; Poloma, *Main Street Mystics*, 65.

108. Åkerlund, "When the Fire Fell."

109. Jacobsen, *Thinking in the Spirit*, 3–4.

110. Poloma and Hood, *Blood and Fire*, 197.

111. Wacker, *Heaven Below*, 266.

organizational structure.[112] On one side, there are stronger inclinations to accept and follow charismatic-type leaders in Pentecostalism than in other Christian tradition due to its openness for the supernatural.[113] In this way, structure facilitates agency in the form of strong leaders who can discern and act on God's will for the organization. Yet, while structure allows for strong leaders in Pentecostalism, it also marks its boundaries since leadership is subject to communal scrutiny. Structure is, in other words, simultaneously enabling and constraining.[114]

Åkerlund and Tangen probe this reciprocal character of leadership in an article where they look at charisma from a critical-realist perspective.[115] Rather than treating charisma as an attribute of the individual or the situation, they suggest that all partners in the leadership relation bear responsibility for avoiding destructive charismatic cultures and promoting ethical agency in the organization. The authors agree with those who claim that there are certain characteristics of Pentecostal ideology that pave the way for toxic leadership in the movement, yet they contend that such structures not only enable autocratic charisma, but also constrain it. The leader is "neither the passive puppet of social forces, nor a pre-social self,"[116] neither entirely free nor totally determined, but one who must choose his path within the repertoire of possible identities that the organization makes available. While leaders may set the direction for the organization, Wacker shows that history bears witness to how Pentecostals restrain leaders who push the limits too much:

> Holy Ghost folk encouraged strong leaders. They put up with autocrats when they had to, but loose cannons they would not tolerate. Knowing the limits was part of pragmatism's text too. In the parlance of a later generation, pentecostals constructed a level playing field where men and women of native talent got a chance to show their stuff.[117]

In a similar manner, Hollenweger admits that the call to be a Pentecostal pastor traditionally has been associated with some kind of vision, prophecy, or doubt about the established church, yet "the decisive element

---

112. Poloma, "Charisma and Structure."

113. Heuser and Klaus, "Charismatic Leadership Theory," 168.

114. Hays, "Structure and Agency."

115. Åkerlund and Tangen, "Charismatic Cultures."

116. Archer, *Being Human*, 283.

117. Wacker, *Heaven Below*, 157.

is always that the call is recognized either by the church to which the perso belongs, or else by a new congregation which is founded as a result of the call."[118] There are no self-made leaders; take the Pentecostal congregation out of the equation, and there is no leadership left. Even the emergence of charismatic Pentecostal leaders is—at least in part—the result of convictions and aspirations among followers.[119] In a treatise on the role of women in ministry and church life, the Norwegian Pentecostal pioneer Thomas Ball Barratt asserted, "If the Spirit calls and the church understands the calling, the inspired woman is ready to take on any responsibility in the Christian church."[120] As interesting as the statement may be with regard to the role of female leaders in the Pentecostal movement, the point here is to note the interaction between God's calling and congregational recognition of that calling. In Warrington's words, "Pentecostals have traditionally preferred to allow their ecclesiologies to develop on the basis of recognized gifts that are reflected in people rather than appoint people to an office in the hope that charismatic authority will be later added."[121] With increased professionalization and institutionalizing, the charismatic component mentioned here may lose its significance in favor of other authority bases. Yet, the dialectic relationship between leader and organization is still prevalent because the pastor loses his ability to influence if he gets seriously out of sync with the congregation.

The previous section highlighted how leaders rely on narratives and communication to set direction for the church. The dialectic addressed in the present constituent underscores that the leader not only shapes the congregational idiom or narrative, but also must adhere to it in order to lead successfully. Lindhardt describes the role of narrative practices in the (re)construction of Pentecostal identities, on the individual as well as the corporate level.[122] Personal conversion narratives, in particular, provide the building blocks for Pentecostal self-understandings and the new social reality narrator and listeners inhabit. Narratives are crucial instruments for human agency because they integrate the temporal flow of activities into a whole that may be shared with others. However, Lindhardt argues that the effects of verbal communication depend on non-linguistic factors, such as

118. Hollenweger, The Pentecostals, 483.

119. See Åkerlund, "When the Fire Fell."

120. Barratt, Kvinnens Stilling i Menigheten, 33. Translation.

121. Warrington, Pentecostal Theology, 138.

122. Lindhardt, "Narrating Religious Realities."

an implicit agreement between speakers and listeners regarding the basic premises of the communicative event.[123] In the narration of testimonies, believers do not only construct or reaffirm their religious identities; they also position themselves within the Pentecostal community. In doing so, testimonies tend to follow culturally and organizationally acceptable plots, connecting individual conversion stories to the communal, and thereby contributing to the creation of shared values and realities. Thus, there are certain implicit scripts the narrator must adhere to if his story is to be accepted or approved—implying that "institutions may exercise power over people by providing a restricted formula for the construction of self-stories."[124] In other words, the narrator has some freedom in shaping individual identity and social reality through the sharing of his story, yet he must stay within the limits of the structural script if his testimony is to be considered valid and trustworthy.

Similarly, Hopewell notes how "a pastor moving from one charge to another encounters strikingly different expressions of value and style in the new church. To communicate effectively within the new congregation, the pastor must master its particular language."[125] This description echoes P3's experience of moving to another church where his personality, gifting, and spirituality clashed with the expectations of leadership in the new organization. The story illustrates that the leader must stay within the (often implicit) expectations the organization has for its leaders, as emphasized in implicit leadership theories[126] and social identity theories of leadership.[127] The enigma of strong hierarchical leadership in coexistence with active lay leadership in Pentecostalism, described in chapter 3, may be explained from this reciprocal relationship between followers and leaders in the Pentecostal congregation. If congregants provide the platform for the influential leader, then the dichotomy between strong leadership and active lay participation is somewhat artificial. Once the leader steps outside the parameters of members' support and submission, his leadership is weakened. The leader is trusted and granted influence to the extent that he meets the expectations of the organization, and leadership rests on his ability to define and articulate reality and purpose in a way that is meaningful for the organization.

123. Lindhardt, *Power in Powerlessness*, 129.

124. Lindhardt, "Narrating Religious Realities," 30.

125. Hopewell, *Congregation*, 6.

126. Junker and van Dick, "Implicit Theories."

127. Haslam et al., *New Psychology of Leadership*.

As alluded to in the treatise on Pentecostal tradition above, discussions on the place of charismatic gifts in corporate settings are not only a matter of practicalities but about who gets to define the architecture of Pentecostal identity. Since Pentecostalism is "the experiential branch of Christianity par excellence,"[128] and experiences are a central dimension of its nature,[129] those who decide what experiences or expressions are allowed in worship services exercise vast influence. Leadership in the Pentecostal movement must balance individuals' access to the charismatic Spirit with the need for organizational cohesion. As such, it simultaneously involves liberation and limitation of setting people free to serve based on their natural and spiritual abilities while defining the boundaries within which their ministry should take place. In all this, the leader functions as a broker of reality for the organization in shaping norms and narratives that guide its being and doing in the world. Such an understanding of leadership goes beyond leader-centric understandings of influence commonly used to explore power issues in leadership research.

French and Raven's taxonomy of power bases (i.e., reward, coercive, legitimate, referent, and expert power) is frequently used in discussions that locate power in the individual leader.[130] While this approach has some merit, it neglects more systemic dimensions of power and influence described here as the dialectic relationship between structure and agency. By merely focusing on how the leader influences the organization through decision-making, complex relationships between leaders and followers go unnoticed.

A more promising perspective is to explore power dynamics through the lens of Lukes' three power dimensions.[131] Lukes' first dimension illustrates the behavioral approach proposed by French and Raven, wherein the leader influences followers to do something they would not have done otherwise. Although this dimension obviously relates to decision-making processes in Pentecostal congregation, the second dimension explores more hidden aspects of power in leadership, namely "the power to decide what is decided."[132] This agenda-setting function means that the leader not only

128. Cox, "Personal Reflection," 30.

129. Anderson, *Introduction to Pentecostalism*, 14; Karkkainen, *Pneumatology*, 87–98; Neumann, *Pentecostal Experience*.

130. French and Raven, "Bases of Social Power."

131. Lukes, *Power*. The use of Lukes' dimensions here is informed by its application to leadership research in Bolden et al., *Exploring Leadership*, 75–77 and Schedlitzki and Edwards, *Studying Leadership*, 125–27.

132. Lukes, *Power*, 111.

uses power to make decisions, but more profoundly holds the privilege to decide in advance the issues to be discussed in the organization. This is, for instance, the power dimension at work when the participants in this study promote some initiatives from congregants in congregational meetings but reject others before they reach the decision-making body, or when they encourage and model some spiritual expressions in communal gatherings but discard others.

Notably, Tangen concludes from his material that the most important form of indirect spiritual leadership in Pentecostal churches is the facilitating of contextualized spiritual encounters.[133] By actively choosing on behalf of the congregation in situations where there are several options, the ecclesial leader acts as a gatekeeper and manager of meaning, one who plays a prominent role in shaping collective identity and spirituality. One thing is what the leader openly decides or directly confronts; another thing is what he inspires or subdues.

Such an understanding of leadership matches DePree's famous dictum that the first responsibility of the leader is to define reality.[134] In a ground-breaking article, Smircich and Morgan emphasize the symbolic nature of leadership and the impact leaders can have on followers through their ability to make sense of organizational realities.[135] Their view is that "leadership is realized in the process where one or more individuals succeeds in attempting to frame and define the reality of others."[136] Thus, leadership resides in the social field rather than in the leader, and the interactive processes that people engage in to make sense of situations, in turn, form organizations as networks of managed meanings.

By the nature of their role, leaders are entitled to influence the sense-making of others. However, since different interpretive schemes may emerge, leaders are effective only to the extent that their definition of the situation provides the basis for the actions of others.[137] As such, leadership is fundamentally a social process by which the leader's ability to lead is proportional in the sense that his definition and interpretation of reality make sense to other people. Put differently, "leaders lead by performing an explanatory function for others who in turn exemplify (to some greater or

133. Tangen, *Ecclesial Identification*, 335.
134. DePree, *Leadership Is an Art*, 5.
135. Smircich and Morgan, "Leadership."
136. Smircich and Morgan, "Leadership," 258.
137. Smircich and Morgan, "Leadership," 262.

lesser extent) these explanations in their responses."[138] Obviously, leaders cannot force people to understand situations the way they want. They can only shape meaning, never dictate it.

By providing legitimate tools in terms of categories and framework—spiritual, theological, and cultural—Cormode believes that Christian leaders influence by providing the building blocks others use to make their own meaning.[139] The term "legitimate" is a key word here, and for the discussion on the relationship between structure and agency. Drawing on Swidler's understanding of culture as a repertoire,[140] Cormode suggests that Christian leaders can use cultural resources to construct interpretations of the world as part of their leadership. For such interpretations to be effective, they must be perceived as good and legitimate by the congregants. To be able to change a congregation, then, Cormode insists that the leader must initiate a legitimatizing process so that people make sense of the new reality that the leader is advocating. "In short, meaning-making leaders give people the vocabulary and theological categories to imagine a different way to interpret the world and to construct a new course of action that flows from that interpretation."[141] As evident from the data, particularly in P3's struggle for leadership in a new congregation, the vocabulary and categories used to interpret the world do not follow a one-way, linear path from leader to follower (actor perspective). People's categories are also something the leader must adapt to and take into consideration if his leadership is to make sense (structure perspective).

If, as Cartledge argues, the worshipping life of the congregation forms its communal identity, the leader has great influence of the organization by framing its corporate gatherings.[142] In this regard, Pentecostal leaders probably have more power and freedom than leaders in historical churches where ministry centers on more prescribed roles such as the administration of Word and sacraments. On the other side, the lack of formalized ecclesial hierarchy combined with a strong, pragmatic inclination to that which "works" in the movement means that Pentecostal leaders who are not able to provide viable expressions of meaning that make sense to followers constantly run the risk of having their leadership base undermined. This

---

138. Pye, "Leadership and Organizing," 46.

139. Cormode, *Making Spiritual Sense*.

140. Swidler, *Talk of Love*.

141. Cormode, *Making Spiritual Sense*, 66.

142. Cartledge, *Testimony in the Spirit*, 29.

brings the argument full circle back to the starting point for this discussion: Leadership shapes the organization, but is also shaped by it. Schedlitzki and Edwards sum up Lukes' third and institutional dimension of leadership by maintaining that power

> is not situated within individuals but within the shared norms and values that influence and control individuals' behaviours. The lesson here for leadership is that leaders' actions and behaviours are shaped by the norms and values they share—with their group, organisation, profession and so on—and these are often enforced through institutionalized mechanisms such as organizational competency frameworks and dominant ideals of effective leadership.[143]

In sum, leadership in the Pentecostal organization resides in the conjunction between organization, situation, and individual, making the relationship between them, not the separate components, a gravid unit of analysis.

Adaptive to Context

Albeit the importance of context has been recognized in organizational leadership studies for some time, the notion of leadership context remains conceptually ambiguous and underdeveloped.[144] To clear the ground, context in regard to this constituent primarily refers to the sociocultural environment that surrounds the Pentecostal congregation. The literature review revealed that Pentecostal leadership—as with many other aspects of Pentecostalism—is contextualized in the sense that it takes on forms and flavors from the settings in which it occurs. When Warrington observes the diversity of leadership models within Pentecostalism, he thus argues that choices regarding governmental forms often are related to the context in which a particular movement is formed.[145] The results from the present inquiry seem to confirm this propensity.

The dominant stream of research on culture and leadership treats culture as a determining factor of what is perceived to be prototypical leadership for a certain group of people and consequently what features must characterize a leader if he or she is to be accepted as such to this group. This perspective on cross-cultural leadership characterized Hofstede's original

---

143. Schedlitzki and Edwards, *Studying Leadership*, 127.
144. Schedlitzki and Edwards, *Studying Leadership*, 81–97, 162–87.
145. Warrington, *Pentecostal Theology*, 137.

research on national culture as collective mental programming,[146] and later large-scale global and European studies addressing the link between culture and leadership.[147] The questions for the present work, then, are if a Norwegian leadership model that reflects Norwegian culture and sentiment exists, and whether Pentecostal leadership adapts to this pattern. In regard to the first question, Grenness asserts that there is a distinct Norwegian pitch to leadership, and suggested that prototypical leadership in the country is partly shaped by strong labor laws and the Norwegian triadic model of trustful relationships between employers and employees, between employers' organizations and trade unions, and between these parties and the State.[148] Additionally, cultural values such as high levels of gender egalitarianism and humane orientation together with low levels of hierarchy favor approaches to leadership that promote trust, consensus, egalitarianism, and participation.[149] These aspects are largely shared by the other Scandinavian countries and are referred to as the Scandinavian model, a management style characterized by informality, equality, compressed salary spreads, participative decision-making and change implementation, and quiet persuasion over charismatic dominance.[150] The phenomenological analysis of interview data indicates that Pentecostal leaders in Norway are entrenched in these values as they seek to promote trust, collaboration, and shared decision-making.

However, this is only half of the picture. The analysis further shows that direction setting is a key aspect of Pentecostal leadership, and that leaders hold a privileged position in deciding and defining on behalf of the congregation. This is, of course, not unique for Pentecostal leadership. Asymmetrical distribution of power is a prerequisite for a social phenomenon to be called leadership in the first place.[151] Yet there are indications from the data and extant literature that leadership in the Norwegian Pentecostal movement is moving away from some of the democratic ideals of previous generations. The discussion above on regulations of tongues in public gatherings epitomizes this trend. The question, then, is whether

146. Hofstede, "Motivation, Leadership, and Organization"; Hofstede, "Cultural Relativity."

147. Brodbeck et al., "Cultural Variation of Leadership"; Dorfman et al., "GLOBE."

148. Grenness, "På Jakt Etter en Norsk Ledelsesmodell."

149. Warner-Søderholm et al., "Doing Business in Norway," 40.

150. Schramm-Nielsen et al., *Management in Scandinavia*.

151. Shamir, "Leadership Research," 487.

these developments reflect a break with or adaptation to the context in which Pentecostal leadership is performed. The answer is probably both/ and. In some regards, the accentuation of strong pastoral leadership marks a break away from the egalitarian bend in Norwegian voluntary organizations, hereunder Pentecostal churches. At the same time, the tendency reflects the influence of globalization on Norwegian society and church life.

Selle and Øymyr show how changes in voluntary Norwegian organizations reflect developments on the macro (societal) level, and suggest that centralization of power and increased leader autonomy is part of this larger picture.[152] Further, influence from globalization forces in general, and American leadership paradigms in particular, put pressure on the egalitarian and informal Norwegian leadership model.[153] On top of this, Norwegian Pentecostal churches have been influenced by international currents in ecclesiology, particularly the emphasis on strong pastoral leadership at the expense of congregational democracy in the church growth literature and neo-Pentecostal megachurches.[154] Whether these developments are for good or bad is a question for another study. Here it suffices to say that developments in Norway seem to support the thesis that Pentecostal leadership is adaptive to context.

The discussion to this point has shown how Pentecostal leaders reflect assumptions and developments in the sociocultural environment in which they lead. Beyond this, the phenomenological analysis demonstrates that Pentecostal leaders consciously and proactively engage culture in their attempt to contextualize the gospel to their contemporaries. This observation corresponds with the previous research on Pentecostal leadership discussed under the heading "Diverse and Contextual" in chapter 3, and there is no need to recapitulate the argument here. The following quote by Samuel epitomizes the trend: "There exists among Pentecostals and awareness of particularities of cultures and context and attempts at new forms of enculturation, though the movement of enculturation is toward emerging contemporary forms rather than traditional ones."[155] From this perspective, leaders take context into consideration in performing their leadership and look for cultural appropriate forms to express Pentecostal spirituality. In

152. Selle and Øymyr, *Frivillig Organisering og Demokrati*, 96–102, 273–79.

153. Grenness, "På Jakt Etter en Norsk Ledelsesmodell."

154. Åkerlund, "Pentekostale Former," 195–97; Clifton, *Pentecostal Churches in Transition.*

155. Samuel, "Pentecostalism as a Global Culture," 254.

P4's words, "the Norwegian sentiment is not [like] America. And it has been important for me to understand that." This is arguably an indicator of a more reflective approach to contextualization than the unconscious and unthematized attempts that have characterized earlier generations of Pentecostals and a move that seems to confirm Lord's assertion that Pentecostals are starting to go beyond mere translation models of contextualization to synthetic models that facilitate a two-way transformation of culture and church.[156]

Maurset's claim that Norwegian Pentecostalism has changed from a holiness movement to a marked movement since the late 1970s fits this picture; "the movement appears today as more open and adapted to the society we live in."[157] As with all attempts to contextualize Christianity, adaptive forms of ecclesial leadership come with certain red flags. Wacker points out one such danger when remarking how the upward mobility of Pentecostals in the West has traded some of its prophetic vision for middle-class values. He claims,

> In crucial respects, the Pentecostal movement is less mature today than it was in the early years. Modern Pentecostals do not need to romanticize their past in order to learn from it. The first generations resisted the blandishments of secular society in order to preach a gospel that challenged the culture in more than superficial ways. Modern Pentecostals might recover that vision . . . They might discover that in the beginning, the movement survived not in spite of the fact that it was out of step with the times, but precisely because of it.[158]

The statement reflects Bevans' critique of the synthetic model of contextualization, highlighting the danger of selling out to the host culture and the need to be suspicious about the powers and manipulations of dominant ideologies.[159] The old adage that he who sups with the devil should have a long spoon underscores the need for thorough reflection when drawing from the wells of contemporary culture in leading the ecclesial organization. The relationship between Gospel and culture is very complex, and for Pentecostals who have

156. Lord, "Pentecostal Mission."

157. Maurset, "Frå Helgingsrørsle til Marknadsrørsle," 85. Maurset observes that some (rural) Pentecostal churches in Norway to a lesser degree has changes during this period. As such, the movement is more heterogeneous with countercultural and culture-open tendencies co-existing within it.

158. Wacker, "Wild Theories and Mad Excitement," 28.

159. Bevans, *Models of Contextual Theology*, 94.

been quick to connect with practices that resonate with their surroundings, the need for critical contextualization is imminent. As Clifton's research on Australian Pentecostalism indicates, the search for relevance may flounder into de-evaluation of theology and critical thinking in a culture of pragmatism.[160] Hence, it is crucial for ecclesial leaders to discern what to affirm and what to reject in the current catalogue of leadership insights, since not all that glimmer are suitable for kingdom work. Jesus' statement "you are not to be like that" (Luke 22:26) drove a wedge between the notions of leadership in his days and those in his kingdom, and continues to do so today. Whether Pentecostal leaders are able to keep the movement's spiritual core intact amidst the pressure from society and other confessional positions remains an open question. Whether they should keep on trying, however, is a closed case: Pentecostal leadership is inherently context-sensitive, and the task of congregational leaders is to engage the context in ways that are culturally open-minded yet theologically informed. In that respect, Norwegian pastors may have risen to the occasion.

Involving the Leader's Entire Life

The importance of role modeling and leading by example has been recognized in theoretical perspectives such as economic,[161] self-sacrificial,[162] spiritual,[163] authentic,[164] and ethical leadership.[165] Further, the idealized influence dimension of transformational leadership theory emphasizes how leaders should behave in ways that make them role models for their followers.[166] In summary, these theories share the common theme that leaders are effective only to the extent that they model the change and behavior they want to see in the organization.

Arguably, the emphasis on modeling takes on even greater ethical significance in religious leadership because the trustworthiness of the message is intrinsically linked with the conduct of the messenger. The participants in this study are consciously and painfully aware of this close connection between their leadership and the shape of their life. Their descriptions

---

160. Clifton, *Pentecostal Churches in Transition*, 194–95.

161. Hermalin, "Economic Theory of Leadership."

162. Choi and Mai-Dalton, "Model of Followers' Responses."

163. Fry, "Toward a Theory."

164. Luthans and Avolio, "Authentic Leadership Development."

165. Brown et al., "Ethical Leadership."

166. Bass and Riggio, "Transformational Model of Leadership."

thus confirm the importance of imitation as a central aspect of Christian leadership.[167] Phenomenologically, this imitation is of a special kind since Christian leaders minister out of the peculiar position of both following and leading at the same time—of being after God and before the congregation. Their leadership is, after all, derived.

Inquiries into Pauline leadership in the New Testament confirm the accentuation on modeling in ecclesial leadership and show how this influence strategy has a distinct Christo-centric shape:

> First, in one sense Paul's model of leadership (the model to which he turns) is Christ, supremely depicted as the servant of the Philippian Christ-hymn; secondly, Paul's model of leadership (the model or example which he sets) is his own, albeit imperfect, "imitation of Christ"; and thirdly, Paul's model of leadership (the model which he teaches) is that, in their own imitation of Christ, leaders should direct all believers to imitation of Christ.[168]

In other words, imitation of Paul was important because he followed the example of Christ (1 Cor 11:1). Only because he demonstrated willingness to sacrifice for the community could he claim their allegiance.[169] Only because his behavior amongst his followers demonstrated his good intentions (1 Thess 2:1–12) could he point to his conduct as a model for Christian leadership to be replicated by others (5:12–13). Paul's *telos* was a people "worthy of God" (1 Thess 2:12; see also 2 Cor 3:18; Gal 4:19; Rom 12:2), and to reach this goal, he relied on modeling as the main method:

> Paul encourages believers to examine and emulate him, making modeling one of the key strategies for spiritual growth among his followers (1:5–7; 2 Thess. 3:7–9; 1 Cor. 4:16, 11:1; Phil. 3:17, 4:9). This corresponds with imitation as a prime pedagogical model in the ancient world and makes up the backbone of Paul's model of leadership.[170]

Ecclesial leaders lead not by "lording it over those entrusted to you, but being examples to the flock" (1 Pet 5:3). To do so, they must be able to point to their own lives as a living demonstration of what they want to see in the community: "You know how I lived the whole time I was with you" (Acts 20:18).

---

167. Bekker, "Towards a Theoretical Model."
168. Clarke, "Be Imitators of Me," 359–60.
169. See Åkerlund, "Leadership in Corinth."
170. Åkerlund, "To Live Lives Worthy," 26–27.

Both the biblical literature and organizational leadership theories affirm the importance of observable leader examples for corporate development,[171] and confirm the finding that Pentecostal leadership involves holistic modeling.

Previously, persuasive communication was described as an important constituent of Pentecostal leadership. The current emphasis on modeling draws attention to how verbal communication as a means of influence is undermined if the leader does not walk the talk. As Tangen observes, the Pentecostal pastor is perceived as a leader worth following only to the extent that he models his life according to the biblical story.[172] This finding echoes Gardner's claim that, although leaders influence through the stories they tell, they must embody these stories and seek to inspire their followers by the example they themselves live.[173] As such, the holistic nature of leadership is not uniquely Pentecostal. However, Pentecostalism's inclination to pragmatism possibly puts extra pressure on the Pentecostal leader to "deliver the goods" in order to be recognized as a leader. This could also be the case when charisma starts to fade in settings where leadership predominantly rests on charismatic rather than legal or traditional authority, as is often the case in Pentecostal circles. Anyhow, the emphasis on holistic modeling underscores the all-inclusive character of Christian leadership, in general, and Pentecostal leadership, in particular, and wraps up the discussion by once again drawing attention to the danger of approaching leadership in Pentecostalism in a reductionist and atomistic fashion.

171. Parker, "Pastoral Role Modeling."
172. Tangen, *Ecclesial Identification*, 186.
173. Gardner, *Leading Minds*, xiii, 9.

7

Pentecostal Leadership and Organizational Leadership Research

AN OVERALL OBSERVATION IS that no organizational leadership theory can adequately describe or explain the understanding of leadership derived from the descriptions of Pentecostal leaders among the participants in this study. This is not to say that insights from organizational leadership research are futile. On the contrary, Van Gelder asserts that it is impossible to lead a congregation in a way that takes its context seriously without giving attention to contributions from the social sciences.[1] From a pastoral educator's perspective, Jinkins claims

> Pastors who have also worked integratively and synthetically in the broader vineyard of theoretical studies have the opportunity to discern even more possible angles on their leadership. And this is crucial, because discernment, perception, judgment, prudence and wisdom represent the gold standard of leadership.[2]

Pastors are not only spiritual leaders, but are also managers with responsibilities for results and personnel. For this reason, they could benefit from management theories and be studied from the perspective of organizational leadership, as in the present work. By looking at congregations as organizations, attention is directed toward social interactions and dynamics that easily slip out of focus in normatively oriented ecclesiological discussions about the nature of the church. Rather than perceiving the theological and

1. Van Gelder, *Ministry of the Missional Church*, loc. 1824.
2. Jinkins, "Leadership and Theory," 209.

sociological dimensions of the church as distinct ontological entities, an organizational perspective allows for an integration of theological reasoning and insights from the social sciences in leading the congregation as a visible entity.[3]

The findings of the present work reveal several similarities between organizational leadership research and the kind of leadership described by the participants—such as an emphasis on setting direction, use of power, defining reality, persuasive communication, sensitivity to context, and leading by example. These parallels should be recognized, but in a way that does not conflate Pentecostal leadership with mainstream leadership theories. There is no doubt that models of organizational leadership have explanatory power that could beneficially be utilized to understand and optimize the ecclesial organization. Yet, the interest in organizational leadership research in religious organizations is fairly new, and one should not be oblivious to how leadership and management theories as newfound friends of ecclesial leadership may bring with them curses as well as blessings. Hence, there is need for caution to avoid a wedding of Pentecostal—or any other form of religious—leadership with the dominating theories of the day. Willimon asserts that "uncritically borrowing from the culture's images of leadership can be the death of specifically *Christian* leaders" and draws attention to how the coupling of religious leadership with contemporary leadership theories is problematic because these constructs, often implicitly, reflect sociocultural currents.[4]

In a historical sketch of leadership research, Grint notes how dominating leadership paradigms reflect the ruling ideologies of its time: "What we think leadership is, is necessarily related to the cultural mores that prevail at the time. Thus, what appears 'normal' at the time . . . can often appear extraordinarily naive when considered retrospectively."[5] Obviously, such time- and context-bound understandings of leadership pose the same risk in religious research, as pointed out in chapter 1. This should not, however, relativize the need for thorough reflection on the relationship between the distinct nature of ecclesial leadership and generic leadership research. To uncritically describe ecclesial leadership in terms of a specific organizational

---

3. Askeland, "Menigheten som Organisasjon," 127–28; Hougsnæs, "Kirkesyn og Kirkeledelse."

4. Willimon, *Pastor*, 55.

5. Grint, "History of Leadership," 13.

leadership theory runs the risk of tapping into a larger discourse that is based on different goals and agendas than that of the pastorate.

Constructivist-oriented leadership scholars call attention to how dominant leadership theories not only explicate how to lead effectively, but form often implicit ideals about what leadership should look like.[6] A credulous affirmation of leadership paradigms from for-profit organizations may thus turn out to be a Trojan horse of rationalities that, over time, may prove of little worth or even be damaging to the religious organization—such as problems with cost/benefit calculation and attempts to organize processes that cannot be organized or demands for effectiveness on the expense of the church's basic calling.[7]

So, while acknowledging the need for interaction with organizational leadership research, it is crucial that these theories and perspectives are scrutinized within a biblical-theological framework. From a Pentecostal perspective, Heuser and Klaus argue for "a Holy Spirit critique on any mode of leadership that reinforces routinization, void of the active moving of the Spirit in the daily life of the organization."[8] As an example, Tangen admits that there are affinities between the inspirational motivation component of transformational leadership theory and the leadership observed in growing Pentecostal churches, but that Theo-dramatic leadership is profoundly different because of its grounding in the larger horizon narrative of the Bible.[9] Thus, Tangen holds that the most obvious difference between transformational leadership theory and the leadership he observed in Pentecostal churches is the importance ascribed to spirituality.

My study confirms this conclusion; it is the commitment to God and his purposes that, in turn, develops into commitment to and leadership in the congregation. Since people's relation to the sacred is their foremost commitment, "forms of spiritual leadership are essential to ecclesial leadership to the degree that one should consider spiritual leadership the primary concept, and transformational leadership the secondary."[10] But what about charismatic leadership theory? In chapter 3, I noted the widespread use of the concept in previous studies of leadership and authority in Pentecostal-

---

6. E.g., Alvesson and Spicer, *Metaphors We Lead By*; Meindl et al., "Romance of Leadership"; Schedlitzki and Edwards, *Studying Leadership*, 233–37.

7. See Karle, "Reforming Majority Churches"; Stewart, "Workplace."

8. Heuser and Klaus, "Charismatic Leadership Theory," 172.

9. Tangen, *Ecclesial Identification*, 328–29.

10. Tangen, *Ecclesial Identification*, 334.

ism, yet it has received little attention in the subsequent analysis. This does not mean that it is not there. Rather, its absence may stem from the fact that charisma, in the Weberian meaning of the word, is largely an attributed phenomenon. Consequently, it is not likely to surface in Pentecostal leaders' self-description. An inquiry into the perception of the pastors participating in this study among their congregants could indicate whether these leaders should be termed charismatic, but that is not a question to be settled in this project. What is relevant here, however, is to highlight the potential problem with the extensive use of charismatic leadership theory or other leadership theories in studies on Pentecostal leadership—not because it is wrong but because its dominance might suppress other perspectives and explanations.

Comparative organizational research has revealed differences in the leadership of ecclesial leaders and that of other managers.[11] This confirms the initial skepticism expressed in the introduction of the study against describing Pentecostal leadership solely by means of established theories of organizational leadership. To take for granted that theories derived in one type of organization uncritically can be transposed to another is a problematic conclusion:

> Today, we might characterize this "organizations are all alike" approach as one of extreme decontextualization. If organizations are all the same and if researchers are studying their own special samples, no detailed attention to "description" is required. . . . If investigators can ignore context and assume that "variables" mean the same thing across all contexts, then they can bring very high-powered results to bear on the data. However, is that a safe assumption to make?[12]

At the end of this study, one is inclined to say no to Aldrich's rhetorical question. There are differences and similarities between secular and religious organizations, as well as between different types of religious organizations,[13] and the way ahead is, therefore, to explore and compare these dynamics rather than merely assume that they are similar. In regard to Pentecostal leadership, Heuser and Klaus suggest that certain characteristics of Pentecostal leadership are at least partly due to the ideology which

11. Andersen, "Vicars vs. Managers"; Hansson and Andersen, "Vicars as Managers Revisited."

12. Aldrich, "Lost in Space," 23.

13. Hinings and Raynard, "Organizational Form," 166–67.

shapes the movement.[14] This is why this study has taken the laborious route of discussing Pentecostal characteristics together with insights from organizational leadership research. This is also why a phenomenological approach that probes for meaning has been preferred over quantitative methodologies that rely on existing theories.

Implications for Practice

Polkinghorne contends that a phenomenological study must have an implication section that spells out the significance of the study for practice and policy.[15] This section is an answer to that call and an attempt to flesh out some suggestions based on the findings and discussions. While the primary purpose of the study is descriptive and academic, its findings may improve practice and contribute to the actual leadership of the participants because self-awareness is a crucial element of leadership development. This is in line with Husserl's emphasis on phenomenological reflection as a way to ethical and responsible living.[16] Since the meaning one needs to reflect on is the meaning one takes part in, reflections on lived meaning are crucial to become aware of the—fortunate and unfortunate—practices one participates in and to engage in discussions on how to improve or change this discourse. In other words,

> clarification of an actual lived state of affairs can lead to constructive change because there is often a discrepancy between what we are actually living and what we think we are living. A discovery of this difference and its correction can lead to more authentic living and interaction with others and thus to a better world.[17]

Experience is not self-interpreting, and the points below propose that Pentecostal leaders must continue to reflect critically on both their tradition and their context in order to develop leadership practices that are theologically faithful and culturally relevant. This presupposes a dual competence of skills in both theology and leadership.

Given the contextual nature of Pentecostal leadership, it feels somewhat counterproductive to nail down practical implications of the study

---

14. Heuser and Klaus, "Charismatic Leadership Theory," 167.

15. Polkinghorne, "Phenomenological Research Methods," 58.

16. Zahavi, *Husserl's Phenomenology*, 67–68.

17. Giorgi, "Phenomenological Movement," 77.

in a step-by-step, how-to manner. Rather, in the following I pinpoint three areas of Pentecostal leadership that I find to be in particular need of critical reflection on practice. First, the issue of power needs be addressed more explicitly. In the course of writing this dissertation, debates about toxic and abusive Pentecostal leadership have cast long shadows in Christian and mainstream media in Norway.

Unfortunately, these incidents are not unique in Pentecostalism's short history. Cox points to the fall of televangelist Jimmy Swaggart as an example of how Pentecostal spirituality may be misused in the hands of skilled practitioners with impure motives, "a reminder that the fire from heaven can burn and destroy as well as purify and inspire."[18] The controversies of the American Shepherding Movement in the 1970s further illustrate the potential for control from strong leaders, especially in supernaturalistic settings such as Pentecostalism.[19] McAlpine even claims that experiences of submission and authoritarian leadership are key reasons why tens of millions of adherents have left Pentecostal-charismatic organizations.[20] Although it is not clear what McAlpine's numbers are based on, toxic leadership is without a doubt a problem that frequently haunts Pentecostalism, probably more so than many other Christian traditions. One reason for this is that leadership in Pentecostalism typically is based on experiences of calling, spiritual gifts, charismatic appearance, or perceived anointing—all authority bases that exist beyond human control or accountability. Since the accrediting institution is outside the organization, the community has no mandate to rebuke leaders whom they did not authorize in the first place.

Fortunately, the picture is not that grim in most Pentecostal congregations in Norway, but the emphasis on strong leadership in combination with less democratic structures may pave the way for autocratic leaders here also. Clifton shows how developments in Australian Pentecostalism—a branch of the movement highly influential in Norway—are partly problematic because the new apostolic structures contain neither bottom-up (i.e., congregational democracy) nor top-down (i.e., episcopal structures) accountability, but have replaced the authority of the congregation with that of the leader, especially the megachurch pastor.[21] Clifton asserts that this is challenging not only for those who see no other option than to leave the

18. Cox, *Fire from Heaven*, 279.
19. See Moore, *Shepherding Movement*.
20. McAlpine, *Post-Charismatic?*, 47–49.
21. Clifton, *Pentecostal Churches in Transition*, 179.

church if they disagree with key leaders, but also because the dominance of a small group of people gives rise to the possibility of group bias due to little collaboration and inclusion in decision-making processes. For all the benefits that come from strong and apostolic leadership, one should thus not ignore that

> when local autonomy is combined with the removal of congregational power, the potential for distortion is magnified. . . . None of this is to suggest that the church does not need leadership and nor is it to assert that democratic government is the only or even the best form of organising community life. But it is to make the point that any Pentecostal movement needs to find ways of balancing the vital input of leaders with the recognition that leadership is subject to distortion. It is also to reassert the fundamental Pentecostal idea that the church itself is not constituted by the pastor (or Pope)—it is not "the pastors church"—but, rather, is the body of all Spirit filled believers whose head is Christ.[22]

This statement leads to my second suggestion, namely the need for thorough reflections on leadership in Pentecostal churches, specifically the relationship between leaders and congregants. In a treatise on Pentecostal theology, Chan claims that the popular concept of leadership that portrays the leader as a man or woman with a vision from God reduces the community to passive followers and subverts the biblical notion of the church.[23] The alternative view that everyone in the community hears and communicates from God as part of the body of Christ is right in belief but wrong in conclusion. According to Chan,

> It often results in a purely egalitarian community in which everyone is potentially, if not actually, a mouthpiece of God. The result is contradiction, confusion and finally division . . . if everyone is a leader then there is really no leadership.[24]

The solution, holds Chan, is a proper view of leadership that balances the integrity of Christ's headship of the church and the distinctive roles of ecclesial leaders. Such a stance implies that leaders are important in helping the community define itself and its role in society, but only if they are sensitive to the tradition of the community. Leaders are not to impose their own vision upon the church, but rather articulate what is already going

22. Clifton, *Pentecostal Churches in Transition*, 210.
23. Chan, *Pentecostal Theology*, 17–18.
24. Chan, *Pentecostal Theology*, 18.

on in the community. This understanding corresponds with the notion of leadership as sense-making (as discussed earlier) and emerging perspectives of organizational leadership research described under headings such as follower-centric, postindustrial, and relational.[25] Together these theories signal a shift in focus "from individual to collective, from control to learning, from 'self' to 'self-in-relation' and from power over to power with."[26] The missional leadership discourse indicates that these thoughts also are gaining momentum in ecclesiology and congregational leadership studies.[27]

Does this mean more church democracy? There are no straight answers to that question. Theologians describing and prescribing Pentecostal leadership and decision-making from a Western vantage point seem to advocate more democracy and community involvement.[28] However, observations among the Progressive Pentecostals of the Global South show other options:

> While there is a natural inclination to favor democratic processes, especially among Westerners, there are also some virtues to benevolent autocratic rule. Senior pastors are able to make decisions very quickly if they do not have to submit every idea to a board or congregational committee.[29]

Complex democratic structures may symptomize organizational rigidity and lack of trust in ecclesial leaders, and are unsuitable to younger generations.[30] Further, a necessary break with the heroic "romance of leadership" approach may well lead to an unintended "romance of collaborative leadership," as there are dangers on both sides of the democratic spectrum.[31] What is at stake is to develop workable and accountable models that combine the priesthood of all believers and the equal access to the Spirit with enough space to lead for those who the same Spirit has called and equipped to lead the community of saints. Thus, if one moves away from traditional venues for democratic involvement—be it congregational meetings or prophetic utterings in public gatherings—new arenas must come instead to

25. E.g., Uhl-Bien, "Relational Leadership Theory"; Uhl-Bien et al., "Followership Theory"; Rost, "Moving from Individual to Relationship."

26. Fletcher, "Postheroic Leadership," 650.

27. Åkerlund, "Missional Leadership."

28. E.g., Johns, "Formational Leadership"; Parker, Led by the Spirit.

29. Miller and Yamamori, Global Pentecostalism, 185.

30. Willimon, Pastor, 282–83.

31. Grint, "History of Leadership," 11.

avoid enlightened absolutism and ensure a proper balance between positional leadership and followership. In a culture like the Norwegian—with strong egalitarian ideals, participative decision-making processes, and a highly educated population—the wise leader will have an attentive ear to the perspectives of others and actively work toward the realization of a learning organization where members contribute in the development and implementation of a shared vision.[32]

Finally, there is a need for more explicit reflection and dialogue on the nature of Pentecostal identity. After all, for Pentecostal leaders to be worth their salt, they must not only be leaders but also Pentecostal. The extant literature and phenomenological analysis witness to how hard it is to define Pentecostalism in any monolithic fashion, and suggest that the way Pentecostal leadership adapts to heterogeneous settings is an expression of, not a break with, its essential identity. However, that the Pentecostal tradition is elastic does not mean that it is empty.

The Swedish pioneer Lewi Pethrus held that Pentecostal congregations were constantly in risk of losing their Pentecostal distinctive if they ceased to experience the power and experience of the Spirit on a regular basis.[33] This view corresponds with the accentuation on spirituality and experience previously discussed. Since Pentecostalism is defined more in spiritual than organizational terms, questions regarding Pentecostal boundary markers become pertinent; when does a congregation become or cease to be Pentecostal? This study has short-circuited the question by defining Pentecostalism organizationally through affiliation with the Norwegian Pentecostal movement. On a more phenomenological note, however, the question is more complex and potent because it addresses the very core of what it means to be Pentecostal. This is not the place to settle this issue or to reiterate what has already been discussed previously. It seems necessary, however, to emphasize that issues of Pentecostal identity deserve continuous attention from the movement's leaders, particularly on the often implicit models that shape congregational spirituality. If intense religious experience is a major factor in Pentecostalism's growth, and worship services are crucial in providing opportunities for divine-human encounters,[34] regulations of spiritual gifts or the form of public gatherings are not peripheral matters but expressions of the deeper quest for the movement's soul. If the

---

32. Senge, *Fifth Discipline*.

33. Davidsson, "Pentekostal Församlingssyn," 158–59.

34. Poloma, "Charisma and Institution," 934.

Pentecostal worship service is reduced to a subset of the evangelical seeker-sensitive gathering, the Pentecostal leader is not only choosing among viable options, but is neglecting parts of his heritage. This is not a nostalgic argument for a return to the heydays of the early revival. It takes a clear mind and a warm heart to sift through the heirlooms of the Pentecostal tradition, and the solution is neither a museum nor a garage sale. What is called for is an increased attention to the theological nature of these issues and, in turn, an open and informed dialogue on the shape of Pentecostal leadership and organizing beyond the constraints of pragmatic reasoning.

8

Conclusion and Suggestions for Future Research

IN ADDITION TO THE limitations addressed in the introductory chapter, some aspects deserve attention at the end of the study. One concerns sampling and recruitment. The findings of this work, like most qualitative studies, are dependent upon the ability of the research participants to identify and explicate their experiences. As such, the results are limited by the participants' descriptions of their experiences and the risk that some aspects and nuances of the phenomenon might stay hidden to analysis. Also, there are possible shortcomings in the selection criteria used in the study. To be a pastor is a social position and does not say much about the "pentecostality" of the participants. In this work, it is just assumed that they share certain characteristics of a Pentecostal spirituality or worldview simply because they work in a Pentecostal congregation. This is arguably a bold move to make, as one cannot be sure up front that these leaders indeed adhere to some canon of Pentecostal tenets given the loose and hyper-congregationalist nature of Norwegian Pentecostalism.

Still, the alternative—to recruit participants based on an *a priori* list of Pentecostal criteria—would be equally problematic, since it would run contrary to the elusive character of Pentecostal spirituality and identity. As discussed in chapter 2, it remains futile, even impossible, to provide a strict and narrow definition of Pentecostalism that at the same time accounts for the variety within the movement. Any attempt to search through the roster of Pentecostal leaders to look for candidates who hold certain characteristics would thus imply a forced harmonization that does not take seriously actual differences among Pentecostal pastors. More than that, such strategy would rely on circular reasoning that defined up front what the study set out to explore, namely the meaning of Pentecostal leadership. Looking at the study in retrospect, then, I remain convinced the approach chosen is not only justifiable but also the best available option given the research question posed. This does not mean that it is without flaws. The limited number of participants, for instance, is a possible weakness for the generalization of the results for Pentecostal leadership elsewhere. However, these limitations should not be overstated, since the phenomenological analysis goes beyond empirical data and includes free imaginative variation in its search of eidetic generalization. As such, the findings are neither universal nor idiosyncratic, but typical or general for a group of people. The procedure generates descriptions that transcend the specific experiences on which they are based, and as such the findings should resonate meanings of Pentecostal leadership in contexts similar to that of the Norwegian Pentecostal movement.

This leads to another tension in the study. I argued in the introduction that leadership in different religious groups should not be lumped together as if they were the same, but rather studied on their own terms and in their natural contexts. The goal of the study, it was said, was to describe the essential structure of Pentecostal leadership, not to reduce its complexity or produce any grand theory thereof. This may look like a contradiction in terms, since the explication of essence seems prone to reduce complexity by necessity. Against this, Giorgi argues that, although the phenomenological structure expresses essential aspects of the concrete experiences, it is inclusive of the many variations that these experiences take.[1] It follows that it is capable of being faithful to complex phenomena that unfold over time by going beyond the idiosyncratic to describe general knowledge of the phenomenon. As mentioned in the method section, this does not mean that the general structure is written once and for all. On the contrary, essences are always relational and context dependent and, therefore, open and expandable. It is quite possible that the general structure changes if empirical data change, and for this reason it should be seen as a type of the experienced phenomenon, realizing that other types exist. This provisional

1. Giorgi, "Concerning a Serious Misunderstanding"

nature of the eidetic structure calls for further research, and the remainder of this section briefly discusses some areas in need of more work.

Hinings and Raynard underscore the need for comparative organizational research, both between and within sectors.[2] Although no comparative research has been performed in this study, comparisons between sectors are addressed by relating present findings with the corpus of organizational leadership theories and by discussing leadership in ecclesial settings versus that in secular organizations. There is no need to recapitulate the argument, and attention is instead directed to the need for further research that compares leadership in different religious and confessional settings—according to Hinings and Raynard, "the rather less explored issue."[3] Assumably, certain characteristics described here as constituents of Pentecostal leadership are the same in other ecclesial contexts. For instance, the constituent describing a dialectic relationship between structure and agency is in no way unique to leadership in Pentecostalism, but applies to most—if not all—leadership situations. One might also suspect that this aspect together with the emphasis on communication over position is particularly important in congregational settings where leadership has a more functional role than it does in the traditional churches. Further, the experience of commitment to a higher purpose of derived leadership and a pragmatic stance toward tradition may reflect a free-church ecclesiology where every believer has direct and immediate access to God just as much as it epitomizes a distinct Pentecostal sentiment. To explore whether the general structure detected in this study is uniquely Pentecostal, then, more research is necessary. I suggest that this could have three directions.

First, future studies may explore whether the findings here apply to Pentecostal leadership in other sociocultural contexts. As it stands now, it is hard to pin down which aspects of the Norwegian narrative speak to other settings, and similar research elsewhere is necessary to detect whether the general structure of Pentecostal leadership applies across differing settings. In Aldrich's words, "unless we conduct comparative analyses, we cannot know that these processes are, in fact, temporally and geographically invariant. At the very least, we should request more replication studies."[4] In practical terms, a fruitful starting point is to conduct a similar study in a different context. To maximize variation, promising places are countries

2. Hinings and Raynard, "Organizational Form."

3. Hinings and Raynard, "Organizational Form," 167.

4. Aldrich, "Lost in Space," 41.

in Confucian Asia, the Middle East, or Latin America culture clusters. By choosing participants from one or several of these contexts, one will increase the likelihood of finding descriptions of leadership that differ from the ones surfacing in Norway. Such findings will, in turn, either strengthen the results of this study or highlight the contextual contingency of the general structure described in the Norwegian setting. Either way, it will deepen the understanding of Pentecostal leadership.

Second, comparative research could relate the findings of this study to leadership in other ecclesial contexts to get a fuller understanding of which characteristics are distinctively Pentecostal and which are shared with pastoral leaders in other confessions. There are indications that religious beliefs impact organizational structure[5] and that differing views on issues like Scriptural authority and ecclesial hierarchy shape views on the role and influence leaders should have in the congregation.[6] To further explore these issues, another replicate study could be conducted in ecclesial traditions different from the Pentecostal movement.

Third, multilevel analyses could provide more insight into leadership as a social phenomenon involving more than the leader. The present work probes only one factor in the leadership process: that of the leader. In this regard, it may be criticized for replicating rather than correcting the one-sidedness of mainstream leadership research in addressing the individual leader rather than leadership as a processual phenomenon emerging in the interactions among people acting in context. One must acknowledge that leadership is not restricted to hierarchy or position, but is best understood as a social, reciprocal, and contextual process in which both leaders and followers contribute to the construction of leadership. Still, Shamir's insistence that the leader/follower relationship can never be fully symmetric, as leadership always involves disproportionate social influence, is a valid objection.[7] To study Pentecostal leadership by exploring the meaning positional leaders give to their experience is, therefore, an adequate research strategy, and the results from this project indicate that it indeed can be a fruitful one. Yet future studies could, for instance, examine the experiences of Pentecostal leadership from a follower perspective to enable a deeper understanding of the social leadership process.

5. Dyck et al., "Organizational Structures."

6. Hinings and Raynard, "Organizational Form," 176.

7. Shamir, "From Passive Recipients"; Shamir, "Leadership Research?"

Concluding Remarks

As stated at the outset of the study, there are personal and academic reasons to embark this study. Now that the work has come to an end, it is time to briefly reflect on both. Van Manen suggests that the question is not so much what we can do with phenomenology, but what phenomenology can do with us.[8] On a personal level, then, listening to these leaders' stories has been a moving and humbling experience. Through their experiences, I have gained a deeper understanding and appreciation of leadership in the Pentecostal movement, and the bracketing of personal understandings and preferences has been nothing but a natural response to the insights they have shared. One can only come as a guest into other people's lives, and to treat these words with caution and be fully attentive to the meaning behind their experiences has been a matter of courtesy as much as of academic rigor.

Academically, the study has supported the assumption that there is no grand theory of Pentecostal leadership. This stems from the fact that the two variables—Pentecostalism and leadership—are so equivocal that any attempt to neatly nail them together is doomed to reductionism. Even now, after its first turbulent and awe-evoking century, it is too early to know what Pentecostalism is in the final analysis due to its emerging nature filled with tensions and possible contradictions.[9] The present work has detected and discussed numerous aspects of the movement as they relate to leading and organizing the Pentecostal congregation, but future research will reveal whether these analyses stand the test of time. Regarding leadership, the search for the organizing "Holy Grail, for the heroic figurehead who will sort things out and lead them to the Promised Land,"[10] is futile because leadership is ambiguous by its very nature. Symptomatically, Ciulla summarized a five-year search for a general theory of leadership by an interdisciplinary group of leading US leadership scholars in the following conclusion:

> It takes more than one scholar, discipline, or theoretical approach to understand leadership. The study of leadership forces us to tackle the universal questions about human nature and destiny. For those questions, there will probably never be a general theory.[11]

8. Van Manen, *Researching Lived Experience*, 45.

9. Kärkkäinen, "Re-Turn of Religion," 476.

10. Pye, "Leadership and Organizing," 46.

11. Ciulla, "What We Learned," 233.

Just as no one would claim to have the final definition of concepts such as love or joy, it is unlikely that anyone will come up with the ultimate, final-word analysis of leadership—in Pentecostalism or elsewhere. This, obviously, does not mean that the phenomenon does not exist, but that definitions and explanations are only partial and should be carefully considered and reconsidered, echoing the Pauline maxim that "we know in part . . . we see only a reflection as in a mirror" (1 Cor 13:9, 12).[12] From a phenomenological perspective, the identity of leadership will always be elusive because the totality of its nature is beyond the reach of human comprehension.[13] This may partly explain the lack of unity and coherence in organizational leadership research. While this conceptual ambiguity undeniably poses a threat to the scientific study of leadership,[14] it also says something fundamental about the essential indefinability of the phenomenon and calls for research on leadership that takes context and meaning seriously.

It was a goal for the present inquiry to get a better understanding of the dynamics of Pentecostal leadership, and in this regard the work has proved fruitful. Whether the insights contribute to a richer understanding of organizing and management beyond its immediate context is a question to be pondered in future studies. At this point, it seems safe to suggest that Pentecostalism is fertile ground for explorations into leadership that happens in relationships between organizational members and positional leaders, structure and agency, words and deeds, and spirituality and pragmatism. In all of this, one is tempted to rephrase Bertrand Russell's statement about philosophy to explain how Scripture and spirituality keeps potential contradictions in the movement in fruitful tension: "To teach how to live [and lead] with uncertainty, yet without being paralyzed with hesitation, is perhaps the chief thing that theology [philosophy in original] can do."[15] Further research along these lines may thus represent a contribution from theology in the development of a new philosophical foundation for Management 2.0, as mentioned in the introductory chapter.

Whether the present work has reached its aspirations is a question now being posed to the wider community of leadership scholars and ecclesial leaders. Since the phenomenological method seeks to go beyond the observed to describe essential features of a phenomenon, there is always

---

12. All Bible references are from the New International Version (NIV).

13. Ladkin, *Rethinking Leadership*, 23–28.

14. Blom and Alvesson, "All-Inclusive and All Good."

15. Quoted in Ladkin, *Rethinking Leadership*, 177.

a risk that the researcher will see too much or too little—to merely stay within the realm of the empirical or let the imagination go awry so that it subverts empirical truths. Sokolowski recognizes the danger of letting the imagination running out of control and asks,

> How do we correct mistakes in eidetic intuition? By talking with others about them, by imagining counterexamples, and most of all by seeing how our eidetic proposals conform to the empirical universals we had identified before we reached the eidetic.[16]

The latter part of Sokolowski's advice is heeded internally in the study by explicating how empirical variations among the participants reflect a common *eidos*. The first two points, however, invite other observers of Pentecostal leadership—practitioners and scholars alike—to examine, question, and discuss the findings of this work in search of a more comprehensive understanding of the phenomenon at hand. As such, this research report is both an inventory of insights gained as well as an invitation to ongoing criticism and confirmation. Sanders reminds the phenomenologist that "learning and doing phenomenology is reminiscent of the Augustinian circle: In order to find out, I must already know, but in order to know, I must first find out."[17] From this perspective, the present work does not mark an arrival but instead proposes a more informed starting point for further inquiry into the fascinating landscapes of Pentecostalism and leadership. If the study may serve such a purpose, it is certainly worth the efforts put into its completion.

16. Sokolowski, *Introduction to Phenomenology*, 183.
17. Sanders, "Phenomenology," 359.

Appendix A

A Note on Rigor

I DECIDED TO KEEP discussions on rigor out of the body text to increase readability, and want to address methodological minutiae in a separate section for those of us who find such things interesting. This is that section. Morse et al. remind the qualitative researcher that "without rigor, research is worthless, becomes fiction, and loses its utility."[1] How rigor is attained in qualitative research, however, is an open discussion, as no single set of criteria applies across the great diversity of qualitative (and phenomenological) approaches. In the following, I will thus briefly discuss some aspects that I believe are especially important in the present work.

Reflexivity and Bracketing

An appropriate entry point for the discussion is my role as a researcher and my proximity to the Pentecostal movement. I was not a pastor at the time of the study, meaning that the participants were not my colleagues per se. Still, the Norwegian Pentecostal movement is relatively small, and many of its leaders are acquaintances of mine. This closeness to the phenomena comes with certain problems and possibilities that need to be addressed. On the positive side is knowledge about cultures and informal structures that is tacit for the outsider-researcher. The insider knows the daily life of the organization—its language, critical incidents, and contextual factors among other things that may influence the collection and interpretation of data. On the flip side, this knowledge is a possible disadvantage, as the

---

1. Morse et al., "Verification Strategies," 14.

insider is likely to take part in the same culture and may consequently find it hard to stand back to assess it. Closeness to data means that the researcher may assume too much and probe too little. Having someone familiar doing research may also lead to lack of depth in data, as the respondent may assume that the interviewer already knows or refrain from sharing critical (or criticizing) information because the researcher is too close. Again, these disadvantages may be countered with possible benefits, as evident in Tangen's study on growing Pentecostal churches.[2] Tangen assumed that his status as a Pentecostal pastor would make the participants hesitant to reveal problems, but found the opposite: Respondents who strongly identified with their church were critical to Tangen as researcher, but opened up once they heard he was also a pastor. I had a similar experience in the course of this project. The potential conflict between closeness and distance is hence a two-edged sword that must be properly dealt with, not simply ignored or avoided.

The key here is reflexivity, arguably the most important dimension of qualitative research. In this regard, Coghlan and Brannick's insistence on "epistemic reflexivity"[3]—involving close analysis of researcher's lived experience as well as theoretical presuppositions—come close to the notion of phenomenological reduction. In the words of Ahern, "bracketing and reflexivity are fruit from the same tree" since the first demands the latter and both activities require time, skill, and support to be effective.[4] The notion of bracketing was discussed in chapter 4, and there is no need to repeat the argument here. However, there are differences between Husserl's philosophical reflections and the social scientist's analysis of descriptions of lived experiences, as the latter deals with other people's accounts, not pure reflection. Pragmatic and instrumental compromise is thus needed to apply philosophical ideals in empirical research, leading to various understandings of the term in contemporary phenomenological research. Thus, a few words are necessary to describe the steps taken to reach a phenomenological attitude in this study.

Husserl's motivation to introduce bracketing of past experience was to ensure that critical attention should bear on the present experience, not to forget the past—"to use the epoché means to bracket past knowledge about the experienced object to experience this instance of its occurrence

2. Tangen, *Ecclesial Identification?*
3. Coghlan and Brannick, *Doing Action Research*, 134.
4. Ahern, "Ten Tips for Reflexive Bracketing," 410.

freshly."[5] It is a means—not a goal—to reach certainty. As such, bracketing does not merely belong to the initial stage of a research project, but involves the constant process of hindering preunderstandings from intruding findings and tamper understandings of participants' life experiences.

There is no set method for undertaking bracketing, and simply stating that bracketing was used without describing how the processes deployed in the actual study therefore jeopardizes its scientific contribution. What is called for is a thorough and explicit description of how the researcher has attained a phenomenological attitude through bracketing procedures. Tufford and Newman's conceptual framework is helpful in this regard, as it positions bracketing between the researcher and the study as a mechanism to ensure the quality of the project.[6] In practical terms, the authors suggested the use of memos, bracketing interviews, and a reflexive journal to ensure and enhance bracketing—all of which were utilized in this study.

First, writing research memos throughout the project allowed me to examine and reflect on my engagement with the data.[7] Memos took many forms, yet the objective remained to shed the light of reflexivity on the corpus of data, to keep track of the development of the study, and to jot down epiphanies and insights that might later show themselves useful for the study at hand. Unanswered questions, frustrations, future direction, and emerging insights are good material for analytic memos, together with everything else that relates to the research or the researcher. Tufford and Newman note the paradox that "memoing one's hunches and presuppositions, rather than attempting to stifle them in the name of objectivity or immersion, may free the researcher to engage more extensively with the raw data."[8] As a means to attain phenomenological reduction, I started to write memos during the proposal phase of the study—prior to data collection and analysis—and continued throughout the research project.

Second, keeping a reflexive journal enhanced the ability to reflect and bracket.[9] The reflexive journal parallels the use of a reflective diary to develop bracketing skills in phenomenological research.[10] As a means to

5. Giorgi and Giorgi, "Descriptive Phenomenological Psychological Method," 249.

6. Tufford and Newman, "Bracketing in Qualitative Research."

7. Saldaña, Coding Manual; Tufford and Newman, "Bracketing in Qualitative Research."

8. Tufford and Newman, "Bracketing in Qualitative Research," 86.

9. Ahern, "Ten Tips for Reflexive Bracketing."

10. Wall et al., "Reflective Diary."

open up one's perspective and ask what one takes for granted, this approach involves pre-reflective preparation, reflection, learning, and action from learning. In this study, the journal was used to reflect before, in, and after the interview situation.

Finally, bracketing interviews with an outside source were used to reach the phenomenological attitude in the study. As Ahern points out, the researcher can only set aside things about which they are aware: "The process of bracketing is therefore an iterative, reflexive journey that entails preparation, action, evaluation, and systematic feedback about the effectiveness of the process." [11] While both memoing and journaling provided a space for researcher reflection, they were singular and private events withdrawn from the reflexive capacity of others. By means of bracketing interviews with an experienced qualitative researcher (Hendrik van der Mescht of Rhodes University, South Africa) prior to, during, and following data collection, I sought to increase my ability to reflect over process and findings and detect themes that might elsewhere have hindered me from seeing the phenomenon as it presented itself. [12]

Reliability and Validity

While some discuss rigor under the headings of reliability and validity, others accuse these concepts of having (post)positivistic assumptions and have proposed a different set of criteria for qualitative inquiry instead. Others again have criticized the lack of reflection in implementing these generic qualitative criteria in phenomenological studies, as they were developed decades ago in another historical context when the goal was to communicate difference between qualitative and quantitative research.

Giorgi treats the issue of validity and reliability on several occasions, but warns about difficulties in cross-paradigmatic communication, as the term may refer to different things within different methodologies. [13] In phenomenological research, validity refers to whether the description of a phenomenon truly captures its essence [14] and provides an accurate picture of structural connections and common features manifested in the collected

11. Ahern, "Ten Tips for Reflexive Bracketing," 408.

12. Rolls and Relf, "Bracketing Interviews."

13. Giorgi, "Validity and Reliability"; Giorgi, "Question of Valididy"; Giorgi, "Phenomenology and the Practice of Science."

14. Beck et al., "Reliability and Validity"; Giorgi, "Validity and Reliability."

examples.[15] This is different from the conventional understanding of validity, and Giorgi suggests that, at a minimum, one should put the word phenomenological in before it if one chooses to use it.[16] This suggestion reflects more than terminological hair splitting. Drawing on Husserl, Giorgi insists that, while phenomenology recognizes the presence of subjectivity, it still makes objective knowledge claims.[17] As such, Giorgi's method is nomothetic.[18] Subjectivity and the world cannot be separated, but are reciprocally related. Thus, to eliminate subjectivity, which is equated with scientific rigor in positivistic paradigms, is neither desirable nor attainable. "Knowledge, as a phenomenon in the world, is strictly correlated with subjectivity. Perhaps there are things or events 'in-themselves,' but there is no 'knowledge-in-itself.' There is only knowledge for a human subject who apprehends it."[19]

The point, then, is to understand how correct knowledge can be obtained. For such knowledge to be coined scientific, Giorgi insists that it must be (a) systematic (i.e., different segments are related to each other by laws, concepts, or meanings), (b) methodical (i.e., gained through procedures that are accessible to other scholars), (c) general (i.e., has applications beyond the specific research situation), and (d) critical (i.e., not merely accepted but challenged by a research community).[20] Giorgi's method meets these criteria and enhances the rigor of the current project.

A detected weakness in previous phenomenological research has been a lack of articulation and identification of philosophical assumptions underlying the actual study.[21] By drawing attention to philosophical underpinnings and showing the link between these underlying assumptions and actual research practice, the present work strengthens the internal rigor of the project. Also, the study meets Norlyk and Harder's criteria for rigor in phenomenological studies by identifying foundational philosophical assumptions, articulating key methodological terms and concepts, and explicating how an open attitude is embraced and sustained throughout the research process. Rigor is further strengthened by keeping a decision

15. Polkinghorne, "Phenomenological Research Methods."
16. Giorgi, "Validity and Reliability," 175.
17. Giorgi, "Question of Valididy."
18. Englander, "Interview," 23.
19. Giorgi, *Descriptive Phenomenological Method*, 99.
20. Giorgi, "Theory, Practice, and Evaluation."
21. Norlyk and Harder, "What Makes a Phenomenological Study," 427.

trail to warrant transparency about decisions made throughout the project and by establishing explicit and sequential steps that may be replicated by others.

As a measure to confer the validity of the research, Walters suggests that participants should be included in the data analysis.[22] This is a step frequently used in phenomenological studies[23] and recommended by some phenomenologists.[24] However, Giorgi argues strongly against the use of participants as evaluators within phenomenology.[25] Such a practice is theoretically indefensible, holds Giorgi, as it overlooks the fact that participants describe experience from the perspective of the natural attitude, whereas analysis is conducted from a phenomenological perspective. Furthermore, Giorgi claims that there is a difference between the experience and the meaning of that experience, and it is not safe to assume that the experiencer is the best judge of that meaning. From a practical perspective, the use of participant feedback as a validity check also undermines the need for any thorough procedure; if the experiencer has the final word, why not simply accept what he or she says without bothering with lengthy analyses? As the study follows Giorgi's descriptive method, participant evaluation or external judges were not used in the analysis.

22. Walters, "Phenomenological Movement."

23. Norlyk and Harder, "What Makes a Phenomenological Study," 428.

24. Bradbury-Jones et al., "Participant Feedback"; Hycner, "Some Guidelines," 291–92.

25. Giorgi, "Concerning Variations"; Giorgi, "Difficulties Encountered"; Giorgi, "Phenomenology and the Practice of Science."

Appendix B

Illustration of Research Method

THE MATERIAL BELOW IS included to illustrate the steps in data analysis following Giorgi's descriptive phenomenological method.

Step 1: Reading of Transcription to Get a Sense of the Whole

Participant 4 (P4): So I have a social contract with my closest co-workers concerning deadlines. If we come to a point where I sense [that] the Lord doesn't say anything, I don't see it clearly, then I am allowed to say so. My closest colleagues cooperate with this spiritual sensitivity. This must not make me kind of. . . it must not make me so important that it's awkward for people. I shall not use it as a form of power. But one example: If we have a "Big Idea"-meeting—a meeting with the preachers in the church—and I was supposed to have nine weeks ready but I only have four, there is an acceptance in the team that it's okay that I only see four weeks ahead. That has been extremely important and many of my closest co-workers have had to learn that. We must respect the inner clock of the pastor. For it will be good in the end, but it is not always we who decide the timing.

Interviewer: How was the relationship between you and the organization, your closest co-workers, in actually leading?

P4: It works in the way that those who are the closest to me understand the most. So for instance when I should explain the series that starts on May 1 and lasts until mid-June a couple of days ago, I do not have anything in writing—I usually do, but this was quite fresh for me—so I only give an oral presentation. Then one of the fellow workers states, "I do not understand where you want to go." And one of the closest associates picks up on my idea and says, "let us try to look at it from this angle," because he is more familiar with how I think. He also knows that confronting that I do not know, does not contribute to a good process. So my experience is that when we are the people of the Spirit, we have another language than just the rational between us. We have an understanding of the spiritual dimension, that we live with a kind of incompleteness that we are not afraid of.

Step 2: Determination of Meaning Units

P4: So I have a social contract with my closest co-workers concerning deadlines. If we come to a point where I sense [that] the Lord doesn't say anything, I don't see it clearly, then I am allowed to say so. My closest colleagues cooperate with this spiritual sensitivity. / This must not make me kind of. . . it must not make me so important that it's awkward for people. I shall not use it as a form of power. But one example: If we have a "Big Idea"-meeting—a meeting with the preachers in the church—and I was supposed to have nine weeks ready but I only have four, there is an acceptance in the team that it's okay that I only see four weeks ahead. That has been extremely important and many of my closest co-workers have had to learn that. We must respect the inner clock of the pastor. For it will be good in the end, but it is not always we who decide the timing /.

Interviewer: How was the relationship between you and the organization, your closest co-workers, in actually leading?

P4: It works in the way that those who are the closest to me understand the most. So for instance when I should explain the series that starts on May 1 and lasts until mid-June a couple of days ago, I do not have anything in writing—I usually do, but this was quite fresh for me—so I only give an oral presentation. Then one of the fellow workers states, "I do not understand where you want to go." And one of the closest associates pick up on my idea and says, "let us try to look at it from this angle," because he is more familiar with how I think. He also knows that confronting that I do not know, does not contribute to a good process. / So my experience is that when we are the people of the Spirit, we have another language than just the rational between us. We have an understanding of the spiritual dimension, that we live with a kind of incompleteness that we are not afraid of.

Step 3: Transformation into Phenomenologically Sensitive Expressions

Meaning Units	Transformed Meaning Units	Further Transformations
P4: So I have a social contract with my closest co-workers concerning deadlines. If we come to a point where I sense [that] the Lord doesn't say anything, I don't see it clearly, then I am allowed to say so. My closest colleagues cooperate with this spiritual sensitivity.	P4 has an agreement with his closest co-workers that, even though they have deadlines, he has the right to say that he does not sense where God is leading them. This way he avoids conflict with his inner compass to convince others. Further, this understanding fosters a corporation in the organization in protecting and listening to the leader's spiritual sensitivity. To cultivate the inner life that is necessary to hear from God for the organization thus does not rest on leader alone, but gets support from the organizational environment.	To hear from God does not only rest on the leader's ability to protect his inner life, but also on the organization's willingness to give the pastor the space he needs to discern what God is saying. P4's leadership is constituted in fellowship where co-workers allows for and empowers P4 to hear from God on behalf of the organization. As such, leadership is, at least in part, an attributed phenomenon in which the leader bases his influence on how other people perceive his connection with God—on trust between leader and followers cultivated in a context of shared and collective spirituality.
This must not make me kind of . . . it must not make me so important that it's awkward for people. I shall not use it as a form of power. But one example: If we have a "Big Idea"-meeting—a meeting with the preachers in the church—and I was supposed to have nine weeks ready but I only have four, there is an acceptance in the team that it's okay that I only see four weeks ahead. That has been extremely important and many of my closest co-workers have had to learn that. We must respect the inner clock of the pastor. For it will be good in the end, but it is not always we who decide the timing.	In P4's experience, the agenda or timeframe is not something the leader sets, but something he receives. P4 describes how it has been crucial for him that his fellow workers accept and remain flexible in relation to his intuition—and that this is something the organization has to learn. God speaks primarily to the lead pastor about the direction of the organization—yet the space to hear from God is constituted by the pastor and other leaders in community.	

Meaning Units	Transformed Meaning Units	Further Transformations
Interviewer: How was the relationship between you and the organization, your closest co-workers, in actually leading? P4: It works in the way that those who are the closest to me understand the most. So for instance when I should explain the series that starts on May 1 and lasts until mid-June a couple of days ago, I do not have anything in writing—I usually do, but this was quite fresh for me—so I only give an oral presentation. Then one of the fellow workers states, "I do not understand where you want to go." And one of the closest associates pick up on my idea and says, "let us try to look at it from this angle," because he is more familiar with how I think. He also knows that confronting that I do not know, does not contribute to a good process.	Answering a question about leading in community with others, P4 tells about how his closest associates knows how he thinks and works, and are able to communicate this to others. Also, they have respect for his inner processes.	
So my experience is that when we are the people of the Spirit, we have another language than just the rational between us. We have an understanding of the spiritual dimension, that we live with a kind of incompleteness that we are not afraid of.	For P4, leadership in Pentecostalism entails that leaders and followers together share an intuitive form of communication that goes beyond the mere rational. It is a shared spirituality, which creates reciprocal trust and understanding of being in process. Since the spiritual dimension is something that the leader cannot control but must submit to, Pentecostal leadership is, for P4, characterized by certain incompleteness that both leader and organization must live with.	

Bibliography

Aburdene, Patricia. *Megatrends 2010: The Rise of Conscious Capitalism*. Charlottesville, VA: Hampton, 2007.

Ahern, Kathryn J. "Ten Tips for Reflexive Bracketing." *Qualitative Health Research* 9.3 (1999) 407–11. https://doi.org/10.1177/104973239900900309.

Åkerlund, Truls. "Leadership in Corinth: Reciprocity and Leader-Member Exchange in 2 Corinthians 6:11-13." *Journal of Biblical Perspectives in Leadership* 6.1 (2014) 162–75.

———. "Missional Leadership: A Critical Review of the Research Literature." *Australasian Pentecostal Studies* 18 (2016). http://aps-journal.com/aps/index.php/APS/article/view/9493.

———. "Pentekostale Former for Ledelse i Fortid og Framtid." In *Pentekostale Perspektiver*, edited by Karl Inge Tangen and Knut-Willy Sæther, 23:187–202. Kyrkjefag Profil. Bergen, Norway: Fagbokforlaget, 2015.

———. "Preaching as Christian Leadership: The Story, the Sermon, and the Prophetic Imagination." *Journal of Religious Leadership* 13.1 (2014) 79–97.

———. "Son, Sent, and Servant: Johannine Perspectives on Servant Leadership Theory." *Scandinavian Journal of Leadership and Theology* 2 (2015). http://sjlt-journal.com/no2/son-sent-and-servant/.

———. "'To Live Lives Worthy of God': Leadership and Spiritual Formation in 1 Thessalonians 2:1–12." *Journal of Spiritual Formation & Soul Care* 9.1 (2016) 18–34.

———. "'When the Fire Fell': Historical and Narrative Perspectives on the Charismatic Leadership of T. B. Barratt." *PentecoStudies* 15.1 (2016) 7–24.

Åkerlund, Truls, and Karl Inge Tangen. "Charismatic Cultures: Another Shadow Side Confessed." Pneuma 40. 1–2 (2018) 109–29.

Albrecht, Daniel E. *Rites in the Spirit: A Ritual Approach to Pentecostal/Charismatic Spirituality*. Journal of Pentecostal Theology. Supplement Series 17. Sheffield, UK: Sheffield Academic, 1999.

Albrecht, Daniel E., and Evan B. Howard. "Pentecostal Spirituality." In *The Cambridge Companion to Pentecostalism*, edited by Cecil M. Robeck Jr. and Amos Yong, 235–53. Cambridge: Cambridge University Press, 2014. http://universitypublishingonline.org/ref/id/companions/CCO9780511910111A021.

Aldrich, Howard E. "Lost in Space, Out of Time: Why and How We Should Study Organizations Comparatively." In *Studying Differences between Organizations: Comparative Approaches to Organizational Research*, edited by Brayden G. King et al., 26:21–44. Bingley, UK: Emerald.

Alexander, Estrelda, and Amos Yong, eds. *Philip's Daughters: Women in Pentecostal-Charismatic Leadership*. Eugene, OR: Pickwick, 2008.

Alvarsson, Jan-Åke. "The Development of Pentecostalism in Scandinavian Countries." In *European Pentecostalism*, edited by Anne E. Dyer and William K. Kay, 7:19–39. Global Pentecostal and Charismatic Studies. Leiden, Netherlands: Brill, 2011.

Alvesson, Mats, and André Spicer. *Metaphors We Lead By: Understanding Leadership in the Real World*. London: Routledge, 2011.

Andersen, Jon Aarum. "Vicars vs. Managers: Do Vicars Differ From Managers in Terms of Leadership Behaviour?" *Journal of Management, Spirituality & Religion* 1.2 (2004) 201–23. https://doi.org/10.1080/14766080409518556.

Anderson, Allan. *An Introduction to Pentecostalism: Global Charismatic Christianity*. Cambridge: Cambridge University Press, 2004.

———. "Patterns in Pentecostal and Charismatic Missions." In *Den Pentekostale Bevægelse*, edited by Mogens S. Mogensen, 19:9–28. Ny Mission. Copenhagen, Denmark: Unitas, 2010.

———. "Signs and Blunders: Pentecostal Mission Issues at 'Home and Abroad' in the Twentieth Century." *Journal of Asian Mission* 2.2 (2000) 193–210.

———. *Spreading Fires: The Missionary Nature of Early Pentecostalism*. London: SCM, 2007.

———. *To the Ends of the Earth: Pentecostalism and the Transformation of World Christianity*. Oxford Studies in World Christianity. New York: Oxford University Press, 2013.

Anderson, Allan, et al. *Studying Global Pentecostalism: Theories and Methods*. Berkeley, CA: University of California Press, 2010.

Andersson, Greger. "To Live the Biblical Narratives: Pentecostal Autobiographies and the Baptism in the Spirit." *PentecoStudies* 13.1 (2014) 112–27.

Applebaum, Marc. "Beyond Scientism and Relativism: Amedeo Giorgi's Commitment to Human Science." In *The Redirection of Psychology: Essays in Honor of Amedeo P. Giorgi*, edited by Thomas F. Cloonan and Christian Thiboutot, 41–60. Montreal, Canada: Les Collectifs Du Cirp, 2010.

Archer, Margaret S. *Being Human: The Problem of Agency*. Cambridge: Cambridge University Press, 2000.

Asamoah-Gyadu, J. Kwabena. "'You Shall Receive Power': Empowerment in Pentecostal/Charismatic Christianity." In *Pentecostal Mission and Global Christianity*, edited by Wonsuk Ma et al., 20:45–66. Regnum Edinburgh Centenary Series. Oxford: Regnum, 2014.

Askeland, Harald. "Menigheten som Organisasjon og Trossamfunn: Organisasjonsteoretiske Grunnperspektiver og Forståelsen av Menighet i Endring." In *Menighetsutvikling i Folkekirken: Erfaringer og Muligheter*, edited by Erling Birkedal et al., 5:115–36. Prismet Bok. Oslo, Norway: IKO-Forlaget, 2012.

Austin, Denise A. "'Decreed by Heaven': A Model for Transformational Leadership in Mongolian Pentecostalism." Paper presented at the Leadership-Biennial International Conference, Alphacrucis College, Sydney, Australia, 2015. http://ac.edu.au/www/upload/documents/2015/July/Decreed_by_Heaven.pdf.

Auvinen, Tommi. "The Ghost Leader: An Empirical Study on Narrative Leadership." *Electronic Journal of Business Ethics and Organization Studies* 17.1 (2012) 4–15.

Avolio, Bruce J., et al. "Leadership: Current Theories, Research, and Future Directions." *Annual Review of Psychology* 60.1 (2009) 421–49. https://doi.org/10.1146/annurev. psych.60.110707.163621.

Barentsen, Jack. *Emerging Leadership in the Pauline Mission: A Social Identity Perspective on Local Leadership Development in Corinth and Ephesus.* Eugene, OR: Pickwick, 2011.

Barnes, Douglas F. "Charisma and Religious Leadership: An Historical Analysis." *Journal for the Scientific Study of Religion* 17.1 (1978) 1–18. https://doi.org/10.2307/1385423.

Barratt, T. B. *Kvinnens Stilling i Menigheten.* Oslo, Norway: Korsets Seiers Forlag, 1933. http://urn.nb.no/URN:NBN:no-nb_digibok_2013031108190.

Bass, Bernard M. *The Bass Handbook of Leadership: Theory, Research, and Managerial Applications.* New York: Free, 2008.

Bass, Bernard M., and Ronald E. Riggio. "The Transformational Model of Leadership." In *Leading Organizations: Perspectives for a New Era,* edited by Gill R. Hickman, 76–86. 2nd ed. Thousand Oaks, CA: Sage, 2010.

Beck, Cheryl Tatano, et al. "Reliability and Validity Issues in Phenomenological Research." *Western Journal of Nursing Research* 16.3 (1994) 254–67. https://doi. org/10.1177/019394599401600303.

Bekker, Corné J. "Towards a Theoretical Model of Christian Leadership." *Journal of Biblical Perspectives on Leadership* 2.2 (2009) 142–52.

Benefiel, Margaret. "The Second Half of the Journey: Spiritual Leadership for Organizational Transformation." *The Leadership Quarterly* 16.5 (2005) 723–47. https://doi.org/10.1016/j.leaqua.2005.07.005.

Berger, Peter L., ed. *The Desecularization of the World: A Global Overview.* Grand Rapids: Eerdmans, 1999.

———. *The Sacred Canopy: Elements of a Sociological Theory of Religion.* New York: Anchor, 1969.

Bevans, Stephen B. *Models of Contextual Theology.* Maryknoll: Orbis, 2002.

Beyer, Janice M. "Taming and Promoting Charisma to Change Organizations." *The Leadership Quarterly* 10.2 (1999) 307–30. https://doi.org/10.1016/S1048-9843(99)00019-3.

Bloch-Hoell, Nils E. *The Pentecostal Movement: Its Origin, Development and Distinctive Character.* Oslo, Norway: Universitetsforlaget, 1964.

———. *Pinsebevegelsen: En Undersøkelse av Pinsebevegelsens Tilblivelse, Utvikling og Særpreg med Særlig Henblikk på Bevegelsens Utforming i Norge.* Oslo, Norway: Universitetsforlaget, 1956.

Blom, Martin, and Mats Alvesson. "All-Inclusive and All Good: The Hegemonic Ambiguity of Leadership." *Scandinavian Journal of Management* 31.4 (2015) 480–92. https://doi.org/10.1016/j.scaman.2015.08.001.

Boje, David M., et al. "Language and Organization: The Doing of Discourse." *Academy of Management Review* 29.4 (2004) 571–77. https://doi.org/10.5465/AMR.2004.14497609.

Bolden, Richard, et al. *Exploring Leadership: Individual, Organizational & Societal Perspectives.* Oxford: Oxford University Press, 2011.

Bradbury-Jones, Caroline, et al. "Phenomenology and Participant Feedback: Convention or Contention?" *Nurse Researcher* 17.2 (2010) 25–33.

Brodbeck, Felix C., et al. "Cultural Variation of Leadership Prototypes across 22 European Countries." *Journal of Occupational and Organizational Psychology* 73.1 (2000) 1–29. https://doi.org/10.1348/096317900166859.

Brown, Michael E., et al. "Ethical Leadership: A Social Learning Perspective for Construct Development and Testing." *Organizational Behavior and Human Decision Processes* 97.2 (2005) 117–34. https://doi.org/10.1016/j.obhdp.2005.03.002.

Brueggemann, Walter. *The Practice of Prophetic Imagination: Preaching an Emancipating Word*. Minneapolis: Fortress, 2012.

———. *The Prophetic Imagination*. 2nd ed. Minneapolis: Fortress, 2001.

Bunderson, J. Stuart, and Jeffery A. Thompson. "The Call of the Wild: Zookeepers, Callings, and the Double-Edged Sword of Deeply Meaningful Work." *Administrative Science Quarterly* 54.1 (2009) 32–57.

Bundy, David. "Historical and Theological Analysis of the Pentecostal Church in Norway." *Journal of the European Pentecostal Theological Association* 20.1 (2000) 66–92. https://doi.org/10.1179/jep.2000.20.1.006.

———. *Visions of Apostolic Mission: Scandinavian Pentecostal Mission to 1935*. Studia Historico-Ecclesiastica Upsaliensia 45. Uppsala, Sweden: Uppsala University, 2009.

Burns, James MacGregor. *Leadership*. New York: Harper & Row, 1978.

Callahan, Sharon Henderson, ed. *Religious Leadership: A Reference Handbook*. Thousand Oaks, CA: SAGE, 2013.

Campos, Roberta Bivar C. "Sharing Charisma as a Mode of Pentecostal Expansion." *Social Compass* 61.3 (2014) 277–89. https://doi.org/10.1177/0037768614535694.

Cartledge, David. *The Apostolic Revolution: The Restoration of Apostles and Prophets in the Assemblies of God in Australia*. New South Wales, Australia: Paraclete Institute, 2000.

Cartledge, Mark J. "Practical Theology." In *Studying Global Pentecostalism: Theories and Methods*, edited by Allan Anderson et al., 268–85. Berkeley, CA: University of California Press, 2010.

———. *Testimony in the Spirit: Rescripting Ordinary Pentecostal Theology*. Explorations in Practical, Pastoral, and Empirical Theology. Surrey, UK: Ashgate, 2010.

Casanova, José. "Religion, the New Millennium, and Globalization." *Sociology of Religion* 62.4 (2001) 415–41.

Chan, Simon. *Pentecostal Theology and the Christian Spiritual Tradition*. London: Sheffield Academic Press, 2000.

Choi, Yeon, and Renate R. Mai-Dalton. "The Model of Followers' Responses to Self-Sacrificial Leadership: An Empirical Test." *The Leadership Quarterly* 10.3 (1999) 397–421. https://doi.org/10.1016/S1048-9843(99)00025-9.

Chow, John K. *Patronage and Power: A Study of Social Networks in Corinth*. Vol. 75. Sheffield: JSOT Press, 1992.

Christel, Virginia A. "The Pentecostal Leader." In *Religious Leadership: A Reference Handbook*, edited by Sharon Henderson Callahan, 119–26. Thousand Oaks, CA: SAGE, 2013.

Ciulla, Joanne B. "What We Learned Along the Way: A Commentary." In *A Quest for a General Theory of Leadership*, edited by George R. Goethals and Georgia J. Sorenson, 221–33. New Horizons in Leadership Studies. Cheltenham, UK: Elgar, 2006.

Clarke, Andrew D. "'Be Imitators of Me': Paul's Model of Leadership." *Tyndale Bulletin* 49 (1998) 329–60.

———. *Pauline Theology of Church Leadership*. London: T. & T. Clark, 2008.

———. *Secular and Christian Leadership in Corinth: A Socio-Historical and Exegetical Study of 1 Corinthians 1–6.* New York: Brill, 1993.

———. *Serve the Community of the Church: Christians as Leaders and Ministers.* Grand Rapids: Eerdmans, 2000.

Clifton, Shane. *Pentecostal Churches in Transition: Analysing the Developing Ecclesiology of the Assemblies of God in Australia.* Leiden, Netherlands: Brill, 2009.

Coghlan, David, and Teresa Brannick. *Doing Action Research in Your Own Organization.* 4th ed. London: SAGE, 2014.

Coleman, Simon. "Transgressing the Self: Making Charismatic Saints." *Critical Inquiry* 35.3 (2009) 417–39.

Conger, Jay A. "Inspiring Others: The Language of Leadership." *The Executive* 5.1 (1991) 31–45. https://doi.org/10.5465/AME.1991.4274713.

———. "Qualitative Research as the Cornerstone Methodology for Understanding Leadership." *Leadership Quarterly* 9.1 (1998) 107–21.

Cormode, Scott. *Making Spiritual Sense: Christian Leaders as Spiritual Interpreters.* Nashville: Abingdon 2006.

Cox, Harvey. *Fire from Heaven: The Rise of Pentecostal Spirituality and the Reshaping of Religion in the 21st Century.* Cambridge, MA: Da Capo, 1995.

———. "Some Personal Reflection on Pentecostalism." *Pneuma* 15.1 (1993) 29–34.

Creswell, John W. *Research Design: Qualitative, Quantitative, and Mixed Methods Approaches.* 3rd ed. Thousand Oaks, CA: Sage, 2009.

Crossman, Joanna. "Conceptualising Spiritual Leadership in Secular Organizational Contexts and Its Relation to Transformational, Servant and Environmental Leadership." *Leadership & Organization Development Journal* 31.7 (2010) 596–608. https://doi.org/10.1108/01437731011079646.

Czarniawska, Barbara. *Narratives in Social Science Research.* London: SAGE, 2004.

Dahl, Tor Edvin, and John-Willy Rudolph. *Fra Seier til Nederlag: Pinsebevegelsen i Norge.* Oslo, Norway: Land og Kirke, 1978. http://urn.nb.no/URN:NBN:no-nb_digibok_2007070404029.

Dahlberg, Karin. "The Essence of Essences—The Search for Meaning Structures in Phenomenological Analysis of Lifeworld Phenomena." *International Journal of Qualitative Studies on Health and Well-Being* 1.1 (2006) 11–19. https://doi.org/10.3402/qhw.v1i1.4904.

Davidsson, Tommy H. "Andlighet och Formative Kontexter: Pentekostal Församlingssyn i Ljuset av Lewi Pethrus' Eckesiologi." In *Pentekostale Perspektiver*, edited by Karl Inge Tangen and Knut-Willy Sæther, 23:153–62. Kyrkjefag Profil. Bergen, Norway: Fagbokforlaget, 2015.

Davie, Grace. *Europe: The Exceptional Case: Parameters of Faith in the Modern World.* London: Darton, Longman & Todd, 2002.

de Castro, Alberto. "Introduction to Giorgi's Existential Phenomenological Research Method." *Psicología Desde El Caribe* 11 (2003) 45–56.

Deininger, Matthias. *Global Pentecostalism: An Inquiry into the Cultural Dimensions of Globalization.* Hamburg, Germany: Anchor, 2013.

Dempster, Murray W. "The Search for Pentecostal Identity." *Pneuma* 15.1 (1993) 1–8.

Dent, Eric B., et al. "Spirituality and Leadership: An Empirical Review of Definitions, Distinctions, and Embedded Assumptions." *The Leadership Quarterly* 16.5 (2005) 625–53. https://doi.org/10.1016/j.leaqua.2005.07.002.

DePree, Max. *Leadership Is an Art.* New York: Doubleday, 1989.

Dierendonck, Dirk van. "Servant Leadership: A Review and Synthesis." *Journal of Management* 37.4 (2011) 1228–61. https://doi.org/10.1177/0149206310380462.

Dorfman, Peter, et al. "GLOBE: A Twenty Year Journey into the Intriguing World of Culture and Leadership." *Journal of World Business* 47.4 (2012) 504–18. https://doi.org/10.1016/j.jwb.2012.01.004.

Drive, Michaela. "A 'Spiritual Turn' in Organizational Studies: Meaning Making or Meaningless?" *Journal of Management, Spirituality & Religion* 4.1 (2007) 56–86. https://doi.org/10.1080/14766080709518646.

Duffy, Ryan D., and Bryan J. Dik. "Research on Calling: What Have We Learned and Where Are We Going?" *Journal of Vocational Behavior* 83.3 (2013) 428–36.

Duffy, Ryan D., et al. "Perceiving a Calling, Living a Calling, and Job Satisfaction: Testing a Moderated, Multiple Mediator Model." *Journal of Counseling Psychology* 59.1 (2012) 50–59. https://doi.org/10.1037/a0026129.

Duke, D. L. "The Aesthetics of Leadership." *Educational Administration Quarterly* 22.1 (1986) 7–27. https://doi.org/10.1177/0013161X86022001003.

Dyck, Bruno. "God in Management: The World's Largest Religions, the 'Theological Turn,' and Organization and Management Theory and Practice." In *Religion and Organization Theory*, edited by Paul Tracey et al., 41:23–62. Research in the Sociology of Organizations. Bingley, UK: Emerald, 2014.

Dyck, Bruno, and Elden Wiebe. "Salvation, Theology and Organizational Practices across the Centuries." *Organization* 19.3 (2012) 299–324. https://doi.org/10.1177/1350508412437073.

Dyck, Bruno, et al. "Do the Organizational Structures of Religious Places of Worship Reflect Their Statements of Faith? An Exploratory Study." *Review of Religious Research* 47.1 (2005) 51–69. https://doi.org/10.2307/4148280.

Easter, John L. "Under the Mango Tree: Pentecostal Leadership Training in Africa." *Pneumafrica Journal* 1.1 (2013) 1–22.

Ehrich, Lisa. "Revisiting Phenomenology: Its Potential for Management Research." Paper presented at the British Academy of Management Conference, Oxford, UK, September 13–15, 2005.

Englander, Magnus. "The Interview: Data Collection in Descriptive Phenomenological Human Scientific Research." *Journal of Phenomenological Psychology* 43.1 (2012) 13–35. https://doi.org/10.1163/156916212X632943.

Ershova, Maria, and Jan Hermelink. "Spirituality, Administration, and Normativity in Current Church Organization." *International Journal of Practical Theology* 16.2 (2013) 221–42. https://doi.org/10.1515/ijpt-2012-0015.

Eskilt, Ingrid. "Misjonærkallet og Kulturens Subjektive Vending." *Norsk Tidsskrift for Misjonsvitenskap* 66.1 (2012) 4–22.

Fairholm, Gilbert W. "Spiritual Leadership: Fulfilling Whole-Self Needs at Work." *Leadership & Organization Development Journal* 17.5 (1996) 11–17.

Faupel, D. William. "Whither Pentecostalism." *Pneuma* 15.1 (1993) 9–27.

Fernando, Mario. "Spirituality and Leadership." In *The SAGE Handbook of Leadership*, edited by Alan Bryman et al., 483–94. London: SAGE, 2011.

Fettke, Steven M. "The Spirit of God Hovered Over the Waters: Creation, the Local Church, and the Mentally and Physically Challenged, A Call to Spirit-Led Ministry." *Journal of Pentecostal Theology* 17.2 (2008) 170–82. https://doi.org/10.1163/174552508X377475.

Finlay, Linda. "Engaging Phenomenological Analysis." *Qualitative Research in Psychology* 11.2 (2014) 121–41. https://doi.org/10.1080/14780887.2013.807899.

Fletcher, Joyce K. "The Paradox of Postheroic Leadership: An Essay on Gender, Power, and Transformational Change." *The Leadership Quarterly* 15.5 (2004) 647–61. https://doi.org/10.1016/j.leaqua.2004.07.004.

Fogarty, Stephen. "The Servant Leadership of David Yonggi Cho." *Australasian Pentecostal Studies* 14 (2012) 42–61.

———. "Transformational and Transactional Leadership in Australian Christian Churches." Paper presented at the World Alliance for Pentecostal Theological Education, Kuala Lumpur, Malaysia, 2013. http://wapte.org/wp-content/uploads/2013/10/Steve-Fogarty-Transformational.pdf.

Føllesdal, Dagfinn. "Husserl's Reductions and the Role They Play in His Phenomenology." In *A Companion to Phenomenology and Existentialism*, edited by Hubert L. Dreyfus and Mark A. Wrathall, 105–13. Malden, MA: Blackwell, 2006.

Ford, Jeffrey D. "Organizational Change as Shifting Conversations." *Journal of Organizational Change Management* 12.6 (1999) 480–500. https://doi.org/10.1108/09534819910300855.

French, John, and Bertram Raven. "The Bases of Social Power." In *Studies in Social Power*, edited by Dorwin Cartwright, 150–67. Ann Arbor, MI: Institute for Social Research, 1959.

Fry, Louis W. "Toward a Theory of Spiritual Leadership." *The Leadership Quarterly* 14.6 (2003) 693–727. https://doi.org/10.1016/j.leaqua.2003.09.001.

Fry, Louis W., et al. "Impact of Spiritual Leadership on Unit Performance." *The Leadership Quarterly* 22.2 (April 2011) 259–70. https://doi.org/10.1016/j.leaqua.2011.02.002.

Fry, Louis W., et al. "Spiritual Leadership and Army Transformation: Theory, Measurement, and Establishing a Baseline." *The Leadership Quarterly* 16.5 (2005) 835–62. https://doi.org/10.1016/j.leaqua.2005.07.012.

Gardner, Howard. *Leading Minds: An Anatomy of Leadership*. New York: Basic, 2011.

Gearing, Robin Edward. "Bracketing in Research: A Typology." *Qualitative Health Research* 14.10 (2004) 1429–52. https://doi.org/10.1177/1049732304270394.

Gibson, Sharon K., and Lisa A. Hanes. "The Contribution of Phenomenology to HRD Research." *Human Resource Development Review* 2.2 (2003) 181–205. https://doi.org/10.1177/1534484303002002005.

Giorgi, Amedeo. "Concerning a Serious Misunderstanding of the Essence of the Phenomenological Method in Psychology." *Journal of Phenomenological Psychology* 39.1 (2008) 33–58. https://doi.org/10.1163/156916208X311610.

———. "Concerning the Phenomenological Methods of Husserl and Heidegger and Their Application in Psychology." In *Essais de Psychologie Phenomenologiqueexistentialle: Reunis En Hommage Au Professeur Bernd Jager*, edited by Christian Thibotout, 1:63–78. Collection Du Cirp. Montreal, Quebec: CIRP, 2007. http://www.cirp.uqam.ca/documents%20pdf/Collection%20vol.%201/5.Giorgi.pdf.

———. "Concerning Variations in the Application of the Phenomenological Method." *Humanistic Psychologist* 34.4 (2006) 305–19. https://doi.org/10.1207/s15473333thp3404_2.

———. "Convergence and Divergence of Qualitative and Quantitative Methods in Psychology." *Duquesne Studies in Phenomenological Psychology* 2 (1975) 72–79. https://doi.org/10.5840/dspp197528.

————. *The Descriptive Phenomenological Method in Psychology: A Modified Husserlian Approach.* Pittsburgh: Duquesne University Press, 2009.

————. "The Descriptive Phenomenological Psychological Method." *Journal of Phenomenological Psychology* 43.1 (2012) 3–12. https://doi.org/10.1163 /156916212X632934.

————. "Difficulties Encountered in the Application of the Phenomenological Method in the Social Sciences." *Indo-Pacific Journal of Phenomenology* 8.1 (2008) 1–9.

————. "The Phenomenological Movement and Research in the Human Sciences." *Nursing Science Quarterly* 18.1 (2005) 75–82. https://doi.org/10.1177/0894318404272112.

————. "A Phenomenological Perspective on Certain Qualitative Research Methods." *Journal of Phenomenological Psychology* 25.2 (1994) 190–220. https://doi. org/10.1163/156916294X00034.

————. "Phenomenology and the Practice of Science." *Existential Analysis* 21.1 (2010) 3–22.

————. "The Question of Validity in Qualitative Research." *Journal of Phenomenological Psychology* 33.1 (2002) 1–18. https://doi.org/10.1163/156916202320900392.

————. "Sketch of a Psychological Phenomenological Method." In *Phenomenology and Psychological Research*, edited by Amedeo Giorgi, 8–22. Pittsburgh, PA: Duquesne University Press, 1985.

————. "The Status of Husserlian Phenomenology in Caring Research." *Scandinavian Journal of Caring Sciences* 14.1 (2000) 3–10.

————. "The Theory, Practice, and Evaluation of the Phenomenological Method as a Qualitative Research Procedure." *Journal of Phenomenological Psychology* 28.2 (1997) 235–60.

————. "Validity and Reliability from a Phenomenological Perspective." In *Recent Trends in Theoretical Psychology*, edited by William J. Baker et al., 167–76. New York: Springer, 1988. https://doi.org/10.1007/978-1-4612-3902-4_17.

Giorgi, Amedeo, and Barbro Giorgi. "The Descriptive Phenomenological Psychological Method." In *Qualitative Research in Psychology: Expanding Perspectives in Methodology and Design*, edited by Paul M. Camic et al., 243–73. Washington, DC: American Psychological Association, 2003.

Glynn, Mary Ann. "Beyond Constraint: How Institutions Enable Identities." In *The SAGE Handbook of Organizational Institutionalism*, edited by Royston Greenwood et al., 413–30. Thousand Oaks, CA: SAGE, 2008.

Gooren, Henri. "Conversion Narratives." In *Studying Global Pentecostalism: Theories and Methods*, edited by Allan Anderson et al., 93–112. Berkeley, CA: University of California Press, 2010.

Greenleaf, Robert K. *Servant Leadership: A Journey into the Nature of Legitimate Power and Greatness.* 25th Anniversary Edition. New York: Paulist, 2002.

Grenness, Tor. "På Jakt Etter en Norsk Ledelsesmodell." *Magma* 4 (2012) 51–59.

Grint, Keith. "A History of Leadership." In *The SAGE Handbook of Leadership*, edited by Alan Bryman et al., 3–14. London: SAGE, 2011.

Gunnestad, Kirsti Thuseth. "Kvinner i Lederskap i Pinsebevegelsen i Norge: En Undersøkelse av Endringer i Synet på Kvinner i Eldste- og Forstandertjeneste i Pinsebevegelsen i Norge." In *Pentekostale Perspektiver*, edited by Karl Inge Tangen and Knut-Willy Sæther, 23:203–20. Kyrkjefag Profil. Bergen, Norway: Fagbokforlaget, 2015.

Hackman, Michael Z., and Craig E. Johnson. *Leadership: A Communication Perspective.* 4th ed. Long Grove, IL: Waveland, 2004.

Hall, Douglas T., and Dawn E. Chandler. "Psychological Success: When the Career Is a Calling." *Journal of Organizational Behavior* 26.2 (2005) 155–76. https://doi. org/10.1002/job.301.

Hamel, Gary. "Moon Shots for Management." *Harvard Business Review* 87.2 (2009) 91–98.

Hansen, Hans, et al. "Aesthetic Leadership." *The Leadership Quarterly* 18.6 (2007) 544–60. https://doi.org/10.1016/j.leaqua.2007.09.003.

Hansson, Per, and Jon Aarum Andersen. "Vicars as Managers Revisited: A Comparative Study." *Nordic Journal of Religion and Society* 21.1 (2008) 91–111.

Haslam, S. Alexander, et al. *The New Psychology of Leadership: Identity, Influence, and Power.* Hove, UK: Psychology, 2011.

Hays, Sharon. "Structure and Agency and the Sticky Problem of Culture." *Sociological Theory* 12.1 (1994) 57–72. https://doi.org/10.2307/202035.

Hermalin, Benjamin E. "Toward an Economic Theory of Leadership: Leading by Example." *The American Economic Review* 88.5 (1998) 1188–206.

Heuser, Roger, and Byron D. Klaus. "Charismatic Leadership Theory: A Shadow Side Confessed." *Pneuma* 20.2 (1998) 161–74.

Hicks, Douglas A. "Spiritual and Religious Diversity in the Workplace: Implications for Leadership." *The Leadership Quarterly* 13.4 (2002) 379–96. https://doi.org/10.1016/S1048-9843(02)00124-8.

Hinings, C. R., and Mia Raynard. "Organizational Form, Structure, and Religious Organizations." In *Religion and Organization Theory*, edited by Paul Tracey et al., 41:159–86. Research in the Sociology of Organizations. Bingley, UK: Emerald, 2014.

Hirschi, Andreas. "Callings in Career: A Typological Approach to Essential and Optional Components." *Journal of Vocational Behavior* 79.1 (2011) 60–73.

Hofstede, Geert. "The Cultural Relativity of Organizational Practices and Theories." *Journal of International Business Studies* 14.2 (1983) 75–89.

———. "Motivation, Leadership, and Organization: Do American Theories Apply Abroad?" *Organizational Dynamics* 9.1 (1980) 42–63.

Hollenweger, Walter J. *Pentecostalism: Origins and Developments Worldwide.* Peabody, MA: Hendrickson, 1997.

———. *The Pentecostals.* London: SCM, 1972.

Holm, Randall. "Varieties of Pentecostal Experience: Pragmatism and the Doctrinal Development of Pentecostalism." *Eastern Journal of Practical Theology* 10 (1996) 31–48.

Holmberg, Bengt. *Paul and Power: The Structure of Authority in the Primitive Church as Reflected in the Pauline Epistles.* Philadelphia, PA: Fortress, 1980.

Hopewell, James F. *Congregation: Stories and Structures.* Edited by Barbara G. Wheeler. Philadelphia. PA: Fortress, 1987.

Hougsnæs, Marit Halvorsen. "Kirkesyn og Kirkeledelse." *Halvårsskrift for Praktisk Teologi* 21.2 (2004) 15–24.

Husserl, Edmund. *Ideas: General Introduction to Pure Phenomenology.* The Muirhead Library of Philosophy. Routledge Classics Edition. London: Routledge, 2012.

———. *The Shorter Logical Investigations.* London: Routledge, 2001.

Hycner, Richard H. "Some Guidelines for the Phenomenological Analysis of Interview Data." *Human Studies* 8.3 (1985) 279–303.

Jacobsen, Douglas G. *Thinking in the Spirit: Theologies of the Early Pentecostal Movement.* Bloomington, IN: Indiana University Press, 2003.

Järvinen, Tomi. "Equipping and Empowering for God's Service: Empowerment: Sociological, Psychological, Organizational, and Biblical Perspectives for Empowering People and Organizations." *Journal of the European Pentecostal Theological Association* 27.2 (2007) 173–82.

Jennings, Jerry L. "Husserl Revisited: The Forgotten Distinction between Psychology and Phenomenology." *American Psychologist* 41.11 (1986) 1231–40. https://doi.org/10.1037/0003-066X.41.11.1231.

Jinkins, Michael. "Leadership and Theory: A Practitioner's Reflection." *Journal of Religious Leadership* 2.2 (2003) 205–12.

Johns, Cheryl Bridges. "The Adolescence of Pentecostalism: In Search of a Legitimate Sectarian Identity." *Pneuma* 17.1 (1995) 3–17.

Johns, Jackie David. "Formational Leadership: A Pentecostal Model for Using the Decision-Making Processes of the Congregation to Nurture Faith." Paper presented at the Twenty-Ninth Annual Meeting of the Society for Pentecostal Studies, Kirkland, WA, 2000. http://www.drawnear.org/formationalleadership/JohnsPaper.pdf.

———. "Yielding to the Spirit: The Dynamics of a Pentecostal Model of Praxis." In *The Globalization of Pentecostalism: A Religion Made to Travel*, edited by Murray W. Dempster et al., 70–84. Oxford: Regnum, 1999.

Johnson, Craig E. *Meeting the Ethical Challenges of Leadership: Casting Light or Shadow.* 5th edition. Los Angeles: SAGE, 2015.

Johnson, Todd M., et al. "Christianity 2015: Religious Diversity and Personal Conduct." *International Bulletin of Missionary Research* 39.1 (2015) 28–29.

Joosse, Paul. "Becoming a God: Max Weber and the Social Construction of Charisma." *Journal of Classical Sociology* 14.3 (2014) 266–83. https://doi.org/10.1177/1468795X14536652.

———. "Max Weber and the Social Construction of Charismatic Power." In *Conference Papers—American Sociological Association* 22 (2009).

Junker, Nina Mareen, and Rolf van Dick. "Implicit Theories in Organizational Settings: A Systematic Review and Research Agenda of Implicit Leadership and Followership Theories." *The Leadership Quarterly* 25.6 (2014) 1154–73. https://doi.org/10.1016/j.leaqua.2014.09.002.

Kaak, Paul, et al. "Integrative Decision-Making for Christian Leaders: Prudence, Organizational Theory, and Discernment Practices." *Journal of Religious Leadership* 12.2 (2013) 145–66.

Karadağ, Engin. "Spiritual Leadership and Organizational Culture: A Study of Structural Equation Modeling." *Educational Sciences: Theory & Practice* 9.3 (2009) 1391–405.

Kärkkäinen, Veli-Matti. "'Culture, Contextualization, and Conversion': Missiological Reflections from the Catholic-Pentecostal Dialogue (1990-1997)." *Asian Journal of Mission* 2.2 (2000) 261–75.

———. "Pentecostal Pneumatologies of Religion: The Contribution of Pentecostalism to Our Understanding of the Work of God's Spirit in the World." In *The Spirit in the World: Emerging Pentecostal Theologies in Global Contexts*, edited by Veli-Matti Kärkkäinen, 155–80. Grand Rapids: Eerdmans, 2009.

———. "Pentecostalism and Pentecostal Theology in the Third Millenium: Taking Stock of the Contemporary Global Situation." In *The Spirit in the World: Emerging*

Pentecostal Theologies in Global Contexts, edited by Veli-Matti Kärkkäinen, xiii–xxiv. Grand Rapids: Eerdmans, 2009.

———. *Pneumatology: The Holy Spirit in Ecumenical, International, and Contextual Perspective.* Grand Rapids: Baker, 2002.

———. "'The Re-Turn of Religion in the Third Millennium'; Pentecostalisms and Postmodernities." *Swedish Missiological Themes* 95.4 (2007) 469–95.

Karle, Isolde. "Reforming Majority Churches: Possibilities and Dilemmas." In *Church Reform and Leadership of Change*, edited by Harald Askeland and Ulla Schmidt, 12:1–17. Church of Sweden Research Series. Eugene, OR: Pickwick, 2016.

Kay, William K. "Apostolic Networks in Britain Revisited." *Pneuma* 38.1–2 (2016) 5–22. https://doi.org/10.1163/15700747-03801003.

———. "A Sociological Perspective on Pentecostalism in Europe." In *European Pentecostalism*, edited by Anne E. Dyer and William K. Kay, 7:383–401. Global Pentecostal and Charismatic Studies. Leiden, Netherlands: Brill, 2011.

Kesseboom, Ingebjørg. "Pinseleiarene Er Redde og Flaue." *Korsets Seier*, October 17, 2016.

Kessler, Volker. "Pitfalls in 'Biblical' Leadership." *Verbum et Ecclesia* 34.1 (2013) 1–7. https://doi.org/10.4102/ve.v34i1.721.

Kim, Kirsteen. *The Holy Spirit in the World: A Global Conversation.* London: SPCK, 2008.

Klaus, Byron. "Pentecostalism as a Global Culture: An Introductory Overview." In *The Globalization of Pentecostalism: A Religion Made to Travel*, edited by Murray W. Dempster et al., 127–30. Oxford: Regnum, 1999.

———. "Implications of Globalization for Pentecostal Leadership and Mission." In *Pentecostalism and Globalization: The Impact of Globalization on Pentecostal Theology and Ministry*, edited by Steven M. Studebaker, 127–50. Eugene, OR: Pickwick, 2010. Kindle edition.

Klaus, Byron D., and Loren O. Triplett. "National Leadership in Pentecostal Missions." In *Called and Empowered: Global Mission in Pentecostal Perspective*, edited by M. A. H. Dempster et al., 225–41. Peabody, MA: Hendrickson, 1991.

Klaver, Miranda. "Pentecostal Pastorpreneurs and the Global Circulation of Authoritative Aesthetic Styles." *Culture and Religion* 16.2 (2015) 146–59. https://doi.org/10.1080/14755610.2015.1058527.

Klenke, Karin. *Qualitative Research in the Study of Leadership.* Bingley, UK: Emerald, 2008.

Kvammen, Per Eivind. "Tungetalen Flyttes." *Korsets Seier*, October 6, 2016.

Laan, Cornelius van der. "Historical Approaches." In *Studying Global Pentecostalism: Theories and Methods*, edited by Allan Anderson et al., 202–19. Berkeley, CA: University of California Press, 2010.

Ladkin, Donna. *Rethinking Leadership: A New Look at Old Leadership Questions.* New Horizons in Leadership Studies. Cheltenham, UK: Edward Elgar, 2010.

Land, Steven J. *Pentecostal Spirituality: A Passion for the Kingdom.* Sheffield, UK: Sheffield Academic Press, 1993.

Lende, Gina. "The Rise of Pentecostal Power: Exploring the Politics of Pentecostal Growth in Nigeria and Guatemala." PhD diss., Norwegian School of Theology, 2015. http://www.mf.no/sites/mf/files/users/Dokumenter/Forskning/Doktorgradsprover/2015/lendetheriseofpentecostalpower.pdf.

Leoh, Vincent. "A Pentecostal Preacher as an Empowered Witness." *Asian Journal of Pentecostal Studies* 9.1 (2006) 35–58.

Levinson, Harry. "Reciprocation: The Relationship Between Man and Organization." *Administrative Science Quarterly* 9.4 (1965) 370–90. https://doi.org/10.2307/2391032.

Lie, Geir. "Fra Pinsevenn eller Karismatiker til Pinsekarismatiker: Norsk Pinsekristendom og Karismatisk Fornyelse fra 1980-årene og Fram til Idag." *Refleks* 8.1 (2009) 64–90.

Lindberg, Alf. "The Swedish Pentecostal Movement: Some Ideological Features." *EPTA Bulletin* 6.2 (1987) 40–45.

Lindhardt, Martin. "Continuity, Change or Coevalness? Charismatic Christianity and Tradition in Contemporary Tanzania." In *Pentecostalism in Africa: Presence and Impact of Pneumatic Christianity in Postcolonial Societies*, edited by Martin Lindhardt, 163–90. Leiden, Netherlands: Brill, 2015.

———. "Introduction: Presence and Impact of Pentecostal/Charismatic Christianity in Africa." In *Pentecostalism in Africa: Presence and Impact of Pneumatic Christianity in Postcolonial Societies*, edited by Martin Lindhardt, 1–53. Leiden, Netherlands: Brill, 2015.

———. "Narrating Religious Realities: Conversion and Testimonies in Chilean Pentecostalism." *Suomen Antropologi: Journal of the Finnish Anthropological Society* 34.3 (2009) 25–43.

———. *Power in Powerlessness: A Study of Pentecostal Life Worlds in Urban Chile*. Religion in the Americas Series. Leiden, Netherlands: Brill, 2012.

Lindhardt, Martin, ed. *Pentecostalism in Africa: Presence and Impact of Pneumatic Christianity in Postcolonial Societies*. Leiden, Netherlands: Brill, 2015.

Lindt, Gillian. "Leadership." In *Encyclopedia of Religion*, edited by Lindsay Jones, 8:5383–88. 2nd ed. Detroit: Macmillan, 2005.

Liu, Caroline H., and Peter J. Robertson. "Spirituality in the Workplace: Theory and Measurement." *Journal of Management Inquiry* 20.1 (2011) 35–50. https://doi.org/10.1177/1056492610374648.

Lord, Andrew. *Spirit-Shaped Mission: A Holistic Charismatic Missiology*. Bletchley, UK: Paternoster, 2005.

———. "Pentecostal Mission through Contextualization." *PentecoStudies* 10.1 (2011) 103–17.

Lukes, Steven. *Power: A Radical View*. 2nd edition. Basingstoke, UK: Palgrave Macmillan, 2005.

Luthans, Fred, and Bruce Avolio. "Authentic Leadership Development." In *Positive Organizational Scholarship: Foundations of a New Discipline*, edited by Kim S. Cameron et al., 241–58. San Francisco: Berrett-Koehler, 2003.

Ma, Wonsuk, et al., eds. *Pentecostal Mission and Global Christianity*. Vol. 20. Regnum Edinburgh Centenary Series. Oxford: Regnum, 2014.

Macchia, Frank D. "Theology, Pentecostal." In *The New International Dictionary of Pentecostal and Charismatic Movements*, edited by Stanley M. Burgess and Ed M. Van der Maas, 1120–41. Grand Rapids: Zondervan, 2002.

Markow, Frank A. "Calling and Leader Identity: Utilizing Narrative Analysis to Construct a Stage Model of Calling Development." PhD diss., Regent University, 2007. https://search.proquest.com/pqdtglobal/docview/304712704/abstract/D331D0EC92194D11PQ/1.

Martin, David. *Pentecostalism: The World Their Parish*. Malden, MA: Blackwell, 2002.

Matviuk, Sergio. "Pentecostal Leadership Development and Church Growth in Latin America." *Asian Journal of Pentecostal Studies* 5.1 (2002) 155–72.

Maurset, Magne. "Frå Helgingsrørsle til Marknadsrørsle? Endringar i den Norske Pinserørsla Sidan 1977." Masters thesis, Høgskolen i Volda, Norway, 2014. http://brage.bibsys.no/xmlui/handle/11250/273583.

McAlpine, Rob. *Post-Charismatic?* Eastbourne, UK: David C. Cook, 2008.

McCauley, John F. "Africa's New Big Man Rule? Pentecostalism and Patronage in Ghana." *African Affairs* 112.446 (2013) 1–21. https://doi.org/10.1093/afraf/ads072.

———. "Pentecostals and Politics: Redefining Big Man Rule in Africa." In *Pentecostalism in Africa: Presence and Impact of Pneumatic Christianity in Postcolonial Societies*, edited by Martin Lindhardt, 322–44. Leiden, Netherlands: Brill, 2015.

McClymond, Michael James. "Prophet or Loss? Reassessing Max Weber's Theory of Religious Leadership." In *The Rivers of Paradise: Moses, Buddha, Confucius, Jesus, and Muhammad as Religious Founders*, edited by David Noel Freedman and Michael James McClymond, 613–58. Grand Rapids: Eerdmans, 2001.

McGee, Gary B. "'More than Evangelical': The Challenge of the Evolving Theological Identity of the Assemblies of God." *Pneuma* 25.2 (2003) 289–300.

McMahan, Oliver. "Spiritual Direction in the Pentecostal/Charismatic Tradition." In *Spiritual Direction and the Care of Souls: A Guide to Christian Approaches and Practices*, edited by Gary W. Moon and David G. Benner, 152–68. Downers Grove: IVP Academic, 2004.

Meindl, James R. "The Romance of Leadership as a Follower-Centric Theory: A Social Constructionist Approach." *The Leadership Quarterly* 6.3 (1995) 329–41. https://doi.org/10.1016/1048-9843(95)90012-8.

Meindl, James R., et al. "The Romance of Leadership." *Administrative Science Quarterly* 30.1 (1985) 78–102. https://doi.org/10.2307/2392813.

Meyer, Birgit. "Aesthetics of Persuasion: Global Christianity and Pentecostalism's Sensational Forms." *The South Atlantic Quarterly* 109.4 (2010) 741–63.

Miller, Donald E., and Tetsunao Yamamori. *Global Pentecostalism: The New Face of Christian Social Engagement*. Berkeley, CA: University of California Press, 2007.

Moore, S. David. *The Shepherding Movement: Controversy and Charismatic Ecclesiology*. New York: T. & T. Clark, 2003.

Moran, Dermot. *Introduction to Phenomenology*. New York: Routledge, 2000. Kindle edition.

Morse, Janice M., et al. "Verification Strategies for Establishing Reliability and Validity in Qualitative Research." *International Journal of Qualitative Methods* 1.2 (2002) 13–22.

Mortari, Luigina, and Massimiliano Tarozzi. "Phenomenology as Philosophy of Research: An Introductory Essay." In *Phenomenology and Human Science Research Today*, edited by Massimiliano Tarozzi and Luigina Mortari, 9–56. Bucharest, Romania: Zeta, 2010.

Murray, Margaret, and Frederick T. Evers. "Reweaving the Fabric: Leadership and Spirituality in the 21st Century." *Interbeing* 5.1 (2011) 5–15.

Myers, Bryant L. "Progressive Pentecostalism, Development, and Christian Development NGOs: A Challenge and an Opportunity." *International Bulletin of Missionary Research* 39.3 (2015) 115–20.

Nelson, Reed E. "Authority, Organization, and Societal Context in Multinational Churches." *Administrative Science Quarterly* 38.4 (1993) 653–82. https://doi.org/10.2307/2393340.

Neumann, Peter D. *Pentecostal Experience: An Ecumenical Encounter*. Eugene, OR: Wipf and Stock, 2012.

Nicolae, Mariana, et al. "The Research Agenda of Spiritual Leadership: Where Do We Stand?" *Review of International Comparative Management* 14.4 (2013) 551–66.

Niewold, Jack. "Beyond Servant Leadership." *Journal of Biblical Perspectives in Leadership* 1.2 (2007) 118–34.

Nooralizad, Rahman, et al. "A Casual Model Depicting the Influence of Spiritual Leadership and Some Organizational and Individual Variables on Workplace Spirituality." *Advances in Management* 4.5 (2011) 14–20.

Norlyk, Annelise, and Ingegerd Harder. "What Makes a Phenomenological Study Phenomenological? An Analysis of Peer-Reviewed Empirical Nursing Studies." *Qualitative Health Research* 20.3 (2010) 420–31.

Osborn, Richard N., et al. "Toward a Contextual Theory of Leadership." *The Leadership Quarterly* 13.6 (2002) 797–837. https://doi.org/10.1016/S1048-9843(02)00154-6.

Oswick, Cliff. "Burgeoning Workplace Spirituality? A Textual Analysis of Momentum and Directions." *Journal of Management, Spirituality and Religion* 6.1 (2009) 15–25.

Parker, Clinton. "Pastoral Role Modeling as an Antecedent to Corporate Spirituality." *Journal of Religious Leadership* 13.1 (2014) 161–84.

Parker, John. *Structuration*. Concepts in the Social Sciences. Philadelphia: Open University Press, 2000.

Parker, Stephen E. *Led by the Spirit: Toward a Practical Theology of Pentecostal Discernment and Decision Making*. Expanded edition. Cleveland, TN: CPT, 2015.

Plüss, Jean-Daniel. "The Frog King or the Coming Age of Pentecostalism." Paper presented at the 9th Conference of the European Pentecostal/Charistmatic Research Associtation, Missionsakademie, Hamburg, Germany, July 1999. http://www.pctii.org/cyberj/cyberj9/pluss.html.

Polkinghorne, Donald E. "Phenomenological Research Methods." In *Existential-Phenomenological Perspectives in Psychology: Exploring the Breadth of Human Experience*, edited by Ronald S. Valle and Steen Halling, 41–60. New York: Plenum, 1989.

Poloma, Margaret M. *The Assemblies of God at the Crossroads: Charisma and Institutional Dilemmas*. Knoxville, TN: University of Tennessee Press, 1989.

———. "Charisma and Institution: The Assemblies of God." *The Christian Century* 107.29 (1990) 932–34.

———. "Charisma and Structure in the Assemblies of God: Revisiting O'Dea's Five Dilemmas." In *Church, Identity, and Change: Theology and Denominational Structures in Unsettled Times*, edited by David A. Roozen and James R. Nieman, 45–96. Grand Rapids: Eerdmans, 2005.

———. *Main Street Mystics: The Toronto Blessing and Reviving Pentecostalism*. New York: AltaMira, 2003.

Poloma, Margaret M., and John C. Green. *The Assemblies of God: Godly Love and the Revitalization of American Pentecostalism*. New York: New York University Press, 2010.

Poloma, Margaret M., and Ralph W. Hood Jr. *Blood and Fire: Godly Love in a Pentecostal Emerging Church*. New York: New York Univesity Press, 2008.

Powers, Janet Everts. "'Your Daughters Shall Prophesy': Pentecostal Hermeneutics and the Empowerment of Women." In *The Globalization of Pentecostalism: A Religion Made to Travel*, edited by Murray W. Dempster et al., 313–37. Oxford: Regnum, 1999.

Priest, Helena. "An Approach to the Phenomenological Analysis of Data." *Nurse Researcher* 10.2 (2002) 50–63.

Pye, Annie. "Leadership and Organizing: Sensemaking in Action." *Leadership* 1.1 (2005) 31–49. https://doi.org/10.1177/1742715005049349.

Rainer, Thom S. *The Book of Church Growth: History, Theology, and Principles.* Nashville: Broadman, 1993.

Reeder, Harry P. *The Theory and Practice of Husserl's Phenomenology.* Pathways in Phenomenology. 2nd edition. Bucharest, Romania: Zeta, 2010.

Repstad, Pål. "Mellom Karisma og Kontor: Pinseledere i Det Moderne Norge." In *Religiøse Ledere: Makt og Avmakt i Norske Trossamfunn,* edited by Cora Alexa Døvig and Berit Thorbjørnsrud, 110–28. Oslo, Norway: Universitetsforlaget, 2012.

Robbins, Brent. "An Empirical, Phenomenological Study: Being Joyful." In *Qualitative Research Methods for Psychologists: Introduction through Empirical Studies,* edited by Constance T. Fischer, 173–212. Amsterdam, Netherlands: Academic Press, 2006.

Robbins, Joel. "The Globalization of Pentecostal and Charismatic Christianity." *Annual Review of Anthropology* 33 (2004) 117–43.

Robeck, Cecil M. "The Origins of Modern Pentecostalism: Some Historiographical Issues." In *The Cambridge Companion to Pentecostalism,* edited by Cecil M. Robeck and Amos Yong, 13–30. New York: Cambridge University Press, 2014.

Rolls, Liz, and Marilyn Relf. "Bracketing Interviews: Addressing Methodological Challenges in Qualitative Interviewing in Bereavement and Palliative Care." *Mortality* 11.3 (2006) 286–305. https://doi.org/10.1080/13576270600774893.

Røseth, Idun, et al. "Engulfed by an Alienated and Threatening Emotional Body: The Essential Meaning Structure of Depression in Women." *Journal of Phenomenological Psychology* 44.2 (2013) 153–78. https://doi.org/10.1163/15691624-12341254.

Rost, Joseph C. "Moving from Individual to Relationship: A Postindustrial Paradigm of Leadership." *Journal of Leadership & Organizational Studies* 4.4 (1997) 3–16. https://doi.org/10.1177/107179199700400402.

Roulston, Kathryn. *Reflective Interviewing: A Guide to Theory and Practice.* London: SAGE, 2010.

Saldaña, Johnny. *The Coding Manual for Qualitative Researchers.* 2nd edition. Los Angeles: SAGE, 2013.

Samuel, Vinay. "Pentecostalism as a Global Culture: A Response." In *The Globalization of Pentecostalism: A Religion Made to Travel,* edited by Murray W. Dempster et al., 253–58. Oxford: Regnum, 1999.

Sanders, Patricia. "Phenomenology: A New Way of Viewing Organizational Research." *Academy of Management Review* 7.3 (1982) 353–60. https://doi.org/10.5465/AMR.1982.4285315.

Schedlitzki, Doris, and Gareth Edwards. *Studying Leadership: Traditional & Critical Approaches.* London: SAGE, 2014.

Scheitle, Christopher P., and Amy Adamczyk. "Divine Callings: Religious Sensemaking in the Organizational Founding Process." *Journal of Management, Spirituality & Religion* 13.2 (2016) 94–116. https://doi.org/10.1080/14766086.2015.1086668.

Schramm-Nielsen, Jette, et al. *Management in Scandinavia: Culture, Context, and Change.* Cheltenham, UK: Elgar, 2004.

Selle, Per, and Bjarne Øymyr. *Frivillig Organisering og Demokrati: Det Frivillige Organisasjonssamfunnet Endrar seg 1940–1990.* Oslo, Norway: Samlaget, 1995.

Sendjaya, Sen, et al. "Defining and Measuring Servant Leadership Behaviour in Organizations." *Journal of Management Studies* 45.2 (2008) 402–24. https://doi.org/10.1111/j.1467-6486.2007.00761.x.

Senge, Peter M. *The Fifth Discipline: The Art & Practice of the Learning Organization*. New York: Doubleday, 2006.

Shah, Saeeda J. A. "Re-Thinking Educational Leadership: Exploring the Impact of Cultural and Belief Systems." *International Journal of Leadership in Education* 13.1 (2010) 27–44. https://doi.org/10.1080/13603120903244879.

Shamir, Boas. "From Passive Recipients to Active Co-Producers: Follower's Roles in the Leadership Process." In *Follower-Centered Perspectives on Leadership: A Tribute to the Memory of James R. Meindl*, edited by Boas Shamir et al., ix–xxxix. Greenwich, CT: Information Age, 2007.

———. "Leadership Research or Post-Leadership Research? Advancing Leadership Theory versus Throwing out the Baby with the Bath Water." In *Advancing Relational Leadership Research: A Dialogue Among Perspectives*, edited by Mary Uhl-Bien and Sonia Ospina, 477–500. Charlotte, NC: Information Age, 2012.

Smidsrød, Åse-Miriam. "'For Such a Time as This': Gender Issues in Twenty-First Century Norwegian and Swedish Pentecostal Churches." *PentecoStudies* 15.2 (2016) 200–220.

Smilde, David A. "'Letting God Govern': Supernatural Agency in the Venezuelan Pentecostal Approach to Social Change." *Sociology of Religion* 59.3 (1998) 287–303.

Smircich, Linda, and Gareth Morgan. "Leadership: The Management of Meaning." *Journal of Applied Behavioral Science* 18.3 (1982) 257–73.

Smith, James K. A. *Thinking in Tongues: Pentecostal Contributions to Christian Philosophy*. Grand Rapids: Eerdmans, 2010. Kindle edition.

Smith, Philip. "Culture and Charisma: Outline of a Theory." *Acta Sociologica* 43.2 (2000) 101–11. https://doi.org/10.1177/000169930004300201.

Sokolowski, Robert. *Introduction to Phenomenology*. Cambridge: Cambridge University Press, 2000.

Statnick, Roger A. "Elements of Spiritual Leadership." *Human Development* 25.4 (2004) 14–24.

Steger, Michael F., et al. "Calling in Work Secular or Sacred?" *Journal of Career Assessment* 18.1 (2010) 82–96. https://doi.org/10.1177/1069072709350905.

Stewart, Alice C. "The Workplace of the Organised Church: Theories of Leadership and the Christian Leader." *Culture and Religion* 9.3 (2008) 301–18. https://doi.org/10.1080/14755610802535645.

Strack, Gary, and Myron D. Fottler. "Spirituality and Effective Leadership in Healthcare: Is There a Connection?" *Frontiers of Health Services Management* 18.4 (2002) 3–18.

Sturgill, Amanda. "Scope and Purposes of Church Web Sites." *Journal of Media & Religion* 3.3 (2004) 165–76. https://doi.org/10.1207/s15328415jmr0303_3.

Sun, Benjamin. "The Holy Spirit: The Missing Key in the Implementation of the Doctrine of the Priesthood of Believers." In *Pentecostalism in Context: Essays in Honor of William W. Menzies*, edited by Wonsuk Ma and Robert P. Menzies, 173–94. Eugene, OR: Wipf & Stock, 2007.

Sun, Peter Y. T. "The Servant Identity: Influences on the Cognition and Behavior of Servant Leaders." *The Leadership Quarterly* 24.4 (2013) 544–57. https://doi.org/10.1016/j.leaqua.2013.03.008.

Swidler, Ann. *Talk of Love: How Culture Matters*. Chicago: University of Chicago Press, 2013.

Synan, Vinson. *The Century of the Holy Spirit: 100 Years of Pentecostal and Charismatic Renewal, 1901–2001*. Nashville: Thomas Nelson, 2001.

———. *The Holiness-Pentecostal Tradition: Charismatic Movements in the Twentieth Century.* Grand Rapids: Eerdmans, 1997.

Tangen, Karl Inge. *Ecclesial Identification beyond Late Modern Individualism? A Case Study of Life Strategies in Growing Late Modern Churches.* Leiden, Netherlands: Brill, 2012.

———. "Et Teologisk Perspektiv på Karismatisk Ledelse." In *Pentekostale Perspektiver,* edited by Karl Inge Tangen and Knut-Willy Sæther, 23:221–40. Kyrkjefag Profil. Bergen, Norway: Fagbokforlaget, 2015.

———. "Pentecostal Movements in Norway." In *Global Renewal Christianity: Spirit-Empowered Movements Past, Present, and Future,* edited by Vinson Synan and Amos Yong, 4:198–214. Lake Mary, FL: Charisma, 2017.

Todres, Les. "Clarifying the Life-World: Descriptive Phenomenology." In *Qualitative Research in Health Care,* edited by Immy Holloway, 104–24. Maidenhead, UK: Open University Press, 2005.

Tracey, Paul. "Religion and Organization: A Critical Review of Current Trends and Future Directions." *Academy of Management Annals* 6.1 (2012) 87–134. https://doi.org/10.1080/19416520.2012.660761.

Tracey, Paul, et al., eds. *Religion and Organization Theory.* Vol. 41. Research in the Sociology of Organizations. Bingley, UK: Emerald, 2014.

———. "Taking Religion Seriously in the Study of Organizations." In *Religion and Organization Theory,* edited by Paul Tracey et al., 41:3–21. Research in the Sociology of Organizations. Bingley, UK: Emerald, 2014.

Tucker, J. Brian. *You Belong to Christ: Paul and the Formation of Social Identity in 1 Corinthians 1–4.* Eugene, OR: Pickwick, 2010.

Tufford, Lee, and Peter Newman. "Bracketing in Qualitative Research." *Qualitative Social Work* 11.1 (2010) 80–96. https://doi.org/10.1177/1473325010368316.

Uhl-Bien, Mary. "Relational Leadership Theory: Exploring the Social Processes of Leadership and Organizing." *The Leadership Quarterly* 17.6 (2006) 654–76. https://doi.org/10.1016/j.leaqua.2006.10.007.

Uhl-Bien, Mary, et al. "Followership Theory: A Review and Research Agenda." *The Leadership Quarterly,* 25.1 (2014) 83–104. https://doi.org/10.1016/j.leaqua.2013.11.007.

Van der Mescht, Hennie. "Phenomenology in Education: A Case Study in Educational Leadership." *Indo-Pacific Journal of Phenomenology* 4.1 (2004) 1–16.

Van Gelder, Craig. *The Ministry of the Missional Church: A Community Led by the Spirit.* Grand Rapids: Baker, 2007. Kindle edition.

Van Manen, Max. *Researching Lived Experience: Human Science for an Action Sensitive Pedagogy.* Albany, NY: State University of New York Press, 1990.

Vanhoozer, Kevin J. *The Drama of Doctrine: A Canonical-Linguistic Approach to Christian Theology.* Louisville: Westminster John Knox, 2005.

Vondey, Wolfgang. *Pentecostalism: A Guide for the Perplexed.* London: Bloomsbury, 2013.

Wacker, Grant. *Heaven Below: Early Pentecostals and American Culture.* Cambridge, MA: Harvard University Press, 2001.

———. "Wild Theories and Mad Excitement." In *Pentecostals From the Inside Out,* edited by Harold B. Smith, 19–28. Wheaton, IL: Victor, 1990.

Wagner, C. Peter. *Churchquake.* Ventura, CA: Regal, 1999.

Währisch-Oblau, Claudia. *The Missionary Self-Perception of Pentecostal/Charismatic Church Leaders from the Global South in Europe: Bringing Back the Gospel*. Leiden, Netherlands: Brill, 2009.

Wall, Christine, et al. "Using a Reflective Diary to Develop Bracketing Skills during a Phenomenological Investigation." *Nurse Researcher* 11.4 (2004) 20–29.

Walters, A. J. "The Phenomenological Movement: Implications for Nursing Research." *Journal of Advanced Nursing* 22.4 (1995) 791–99. https://doi.org/10.1046/j.1365-2648.1995.22040791.x.

Warner-Søderholm, Gillian, et al. "Doing Business in Norway: An International Perspective." *Asian Journal of Research in Business Economics and Management* 4.11 (2014) 32. https://doi.org/10.5958/2249-7307.2014.00971.2.

Warrington, Keith. *Pentecostal Theology: A Theology of Encounter*. London: T. & T. Clark, 2008.

Weber, Klaus, and Mary Ann Glynn. "Making Sense with Institutions: Context, Thought and Action in Karl Weick's Theory." *Organization Studies* 27.11 (2006) 1639–60.

Weber, Max. *On Charisma and Institution Building: Selected Papers*. Edited by S. N. Eisenstadt. Chicago: The University of Chicago Press, 1968.

Wertz, Frederick J. "A Phenomenological Psychological Approach to Trauma and Resilience." In *Five Ways of Doing Qualitative Analysis: Phenomenological Psychology, Grounded Theory, Discourse Analysis, Narrative Research, and Intuitive*, by Frederick J. Wertz et al., 124–64. New York: Guilford, 2011.

———. "From Everyday to Psychological Description: Analyzing the Moments of a Qualitative Data Analysis." *Journal of Phenomenological Psychology* 14.2 (1983) 197–241. https://doi.org/10.1163/156916283X00108.

Whittington, J. Lee, et al. "Legacy Leadership: The Leadership Wisdom of the Apostle Paul." *The Leadership Quarterly* 16.5 (2005) 749–70. https://doi.org/10.1016/j.leaqua.2005.07.006.

Wilkinson, Michael. "The 'Many Tongues' of Global Pentecostalism." In *Global Pentecostal Movements: Migration, Mission, and Public Religion*, 3–14. Leiden, Netherlands: Brill, 2012.

———. "What's 'Global' about Global Pentecostalism?" *Journal of Pentecostal Theology* 17.1 (2008) 96–109. https://doi.org/Article.

Willimon, William H. *Pastor: The Theology and Practice of Ordained Ministry*. Nashville: Abingdon, 2002.

Wojnar, Danuta M., and Kristen M. Swanson. "Phenomenology: An Exploration." *Journal of Holistic Nursing* 25.3 (2007) 172–80. https://doi.org/10.1177/0898010106295172.

Yong, Amos. "Disability and the Gifts of the Spirit: Pentecost and the Renewal of the Church." *Journal of Pentecostal Theology* 19.1 (2010) 76–93. https://doi.org/10.1163/174552510X489973.

Yukl, Gary A. *Leadership in Organizations*. Boston: Pearson Education, 2013.

Yung, Hwa. "The Integrity of Mission in the Light of the Gospel: Bearing the Witness of the Spirit." *Mission Studies: Journal of the International Association for Mission Studies* 24.2 (2007) 169–88. https://doi.org/10.1163/157338307X234833.

Zahavi, Dan. *Husserl's Phenomenology*. Stanford, CA: Stanford University Press, 2003.

Zaner, Richard M. "At Play in the Field of Possibles." *Journal of Phenomenological Psychology* 41 (2010) 28–84.

Zsolnai, László. *Spirituality and Ethics in Management*. London: Kluwer, 2011.

Zuesse, Evan M. "The Role of Intentionality in the Phenomenology of Religion." *Journal of the American Academy of Religion* 53.1 (1985) 51–73.